For Elyssa
from Alex and I
with respect and admi-
and love for a true arte
an observation made with the faith
in you, absolute at first en e-

Alexander Blackbur

10-18-2019

The
Fire Within
Reflections on the Literary Imagination

THE
FIRE
WITHIN

Reflections on the Literary Imagination

Alexander Blackburn

with a Foreword by Yusef Komunyakaa

IRIE
BOOKS

ISBN 978-1-5154-1724-8
Copyright 2019 by Alexander Blackburn

Cover and interior design by Nancy R Koucky, NRK Designs
Front cover artwork
Johannes Vermeer: "The Geographer"

The Fire Within is published by Irie Books, Santa Fe, New Mexico
For information, contact www.iriebooks.com

IRIE
BOOKS

To All Who Have an Incorrigible Passion for Literature

Imagination is more important than knowledge
—*Albert Einstein*

Imagination Dead Imagine
—Samuel Beckett

Those images that yet
Fresh images beget,
That dolphin-torn, that gong-tormented sea
-—*William Butler Yeats,* "Byzantium"

For we move – each – in two worlds: the inward of our own awareness, and an outward of participation in the history of our time and place. The scientist and historian serve the latter: the world, that is to say, of things "out there," where people are interchangeable, and language serves to communicate information and commands. Creative artists, on the other hand, are mankind's wakeners to recollection: summoners of our outward mind to conscious contact with ourselves, not as participants in this or that morsel of history, but as spirit, in the consciousness of being.
—*Joseph Campbell,* **Creative Mythology**

CONTENTS

FOREWORD

Yusef Komunyakaa

Alex Blackburn was one of my most provocative and influential teachers in 1973 when I was enrolled at the University of Colorado in Colorado Springs. And he is still burning the proverbial lamp that burns back to the core of the caldron, to the source, to that individualistic, pragmatic quest for democratic ideas, expression, and lived lives. Hell, no, his is not a conjured Jeremiah voice yelling "fire" in a crowded corridor or rustic temple. Early on, after riffing on a list of influences and literary philosophies in *The Fire Within*, the author declares:

> If we didn't believe that imagination in general and the literary imagination in particular hold us together and are central to human survival, I would not hesitate to omit from these reflections most of the personal notes that resemble a memoir, but a testimonial of sorts is unavoidable. I found the fire within myself, so why not to tell others of this power within themselves, this prophetic soul?

Indeed, Alex trusts the imagination to prod the individual citizen if not into action, then at least into posing the most robust questions—and this is doubly so for the poet or writer.

This son of the South possesses an authentic voice. Perhaps the grace embedded in place took root in North Carolina before the civil rights movement, the ease of movement and symmetry may have been honed in the North, at Yale, and then polished at Cambridge, the music of the telling is homegrown and driven by basic love. Alex gives the reader the whole story through vivid details, with illuminating forays into the complex souls of his characters—portrayals of their arrivals and betrayals.

The Fire Within goes directly back to a query of the soil, to nature, and to the people. While the breath and sound of this voice begin with family, the collection defies the traditional memoir. It does the work, unearths, and then holds up the evidence of Self to natural light but also to the light of tradition. The reader not only senses the hard work, but he or she feels and experiences step-by-step the quest—the journey. This patriotic speaker loves not only the stolen soil and the people but also the heroic dream. He embraces a true freedom that fractures the design of the patriarchy. He bares the double quest in the soul of America.

Blackburn underscores how imagination is the fuse and fuel of national (natural) dreaming. He exposes the veins of his major characters, how each has enhanced his personal journey. He knows how important the question is, how it takes on the inquiring, and at times, ruthless brain.

When Blackburn adjusts his sights on the novelist Frank Waters and on New Mexico where the writer later lived, Blackburn seems carried at least halfway home again—he meets a writer who cares for nature as much as he does, who's at home with the poetry in the soil, the rocks, the creek bed, trees, and animal life, where basic humanity is located. When Blackburn says, "We are already the Other," as he summons his many thoughts on Frank Waters, one feels that he hits illuminated pay dirt. Here, in New Mexico, it seems Alex has met his twin.

When Blackburn exacts the poetry of seeing he simultaneously assays us back to an inherited sense of responsibility. He questions monolithic symbols and systems of thinking that diminish experience and undermine the individual. He says, "Experience is up against Authority. The literary form especially adapted to confront de-humanizing threats, externalized and internalized, is the modern novel, the quintessential technique of which is conflict—a war in which humanity itself is at stake."

It is quite in tune with Blackburn to believe that imaginative writing, especially the novel, cannot be divorced from a full imagination, that creative art it is never merely social journalism, but that the imagination is intricately woven into the making of a creation. The music in language is also an intricate part or facet of the lived and felt journey—there's living breath in this window on the world. He states forthrightly the organized forces that attempt to undermine creative literary imagination:

> In America, the imagination is engaged with forces it cannot hope to defeat, forces such as technology, big business, the military-industrial complex, advertising, public education, professional football, politicized evangelism, teachers, parents, and other organized crimes. These forces are inhospitable to imagination, which at its happiest would find real substance in the world of history and society.

Alex Blackburn, this engaging writer and thinker, does not render the citizens or his characters any inherited privilege or clemency. In fact, out of love, he holds us all accountable—this is especially for our treatment of each other and desecration of the Earth. He rolls out a wide, encompassing series of unforgiving thoughts and lifelines that snare the reader's attention. Blackburn journeys from 12th century lore and mythology to the epicenter of now; he deconstructs dogmas by addressing the importance of literary process and natural inquiry, and then he reveals the false shapes underneath our sense of modernity. One could say that the aim of this mature thinker is to sow seeds of constructive unrest through empirical summons—an echo of Socratic reckoning.

No one wiggles off the hook. But this is doubly true for near the end of this forum of ideas and memoir, *The Fire Within*, when Alex Blackburn, a son of the South, takes us to Charlottesville, Virginia. He speaks directly to the authority that embraced the hellions and their brutal show of force. And then he says, "You, Heather Heyer, exemplify the higher levels consciousness that endow the literary imagination with the authority to lift our hearts in memory of a person in the vanguard of a new world of the mind."

Blackburn's response to the zeitgeist and shortcomings planted in our national psyche, whether "race-fear" or over-commercialization, he is apt and spot on. And his critique is not a blurt into existential darkness after a wild ride of the 6 o'clock evening news as entertainment; in fact, when he says, "Imagination is a force of consciousness, one of the ways we think" this philosophical thinker has mapped a fearless questioning that converges with mindful truths.

I

CHAPTER I

Holding Us Together

Our Gutenberg galaxy of typography with the printed book its brightest star is fast disappearing into a black hole of illiteracy.[1] Enervated by the Internet, bookstores are going out of business, and writers whose books are marketed elsewhere make only a small percentage of what their work should be worth. The case-bound books available in grocery stores are flash merchandise obscenely shelved next to contraceptives and soap. Library books are being transformed into "virtual" files that fit comfortably into a Porta-Potty or a thimble. The personal letter has become a rarity, its emotions now manufactured for us on cards with cartoons, sentimentalized, snide, and sententious. Penmanship itself is being eliminated from the curriculum of schools. As literacy declines, fake spectacles from professional wrestling to presidential elections triumph. As the rough beast of barbarism slouches its way into our minds, a new dark age of the soul is born.

Why, then, bother to read, write, and study literature if these pursuits lack the respect bestowed upon them since ancient times? Need employment in the "real" world? Write conduct literature for the corporate state. The job of producing conduct literature requires writers who tell women to be silent, obedient, and chaste and men to be intellectual eunuchs, cowed by and compliant with the communal order. Of course, some practical concern about the marketable worth of a literary vocation has almost always seemed partially valid, though somewhat hysterical, especially when it is expressed by those who love us and want us to take a primrose path. A writer, no matter how compelled to write, is bound to feel anxious to prove himself a financial success.

Nowadays there is in America a widespread belief that there's a pot of gold awaiting a writer at the end of his rainbow. Recently, for example, during my visit to a little bookstore cleverly named Moby Dickens, a young clerk put her hand over her heart and gushed, "I wish I could write a novel and make a million dollars!" I could have told her that the number of writers who earn a living from their books and articles of fiction and nonfiction is a very small percentage of all American writers. Or I could have told her about my brief encounter with Norman Mailer. He may have made, I believe, a million dollars for his self-advertisements but evidently lost a lot of them paying for alimonies. I was at a party in Greenwich Village at the home of an editor at Random House. I was chatting with Peter Matthiessen, editor of *The Paris Review*. Although I was younger than he, we had mutual friends and felt at ease. As the home was a single-story ground-floor house, straight in from the street stormed Mailer. Brushing Matthiessen rudely aside, he sashayed into an unoccupied bedroom, halted under a dangling light bulb, folded his arms, tilted his chin and waited for idolaters to rush like moths to his lit-up literary light. "I'm leaving," Matthiessen said to me in a clipped accent. "Me too," I said. The literary imagination and the arrogance of solipsism are an unpleasant combination.

Writers continue to get published one way or another, some with big-name publishers, some with small and independent presses, some in the "under-the-radar" and shrinking number of literary magazines. Whereas sixty years ago there were probably fewer than a couple of dozen professors of creative writing and still fewer post-graduate programs in creative writing in degree-granting institutions, today there are over 800 such programs staffed by veteran poets and writers. Where a yearning for riches through writing is concerned, I'm afraid we should set aside our inspirational copies of *Writer's Digest*, our admiration for Stephen King, Tom Clancy, and J.K. Rowling, and our fantasy of writers as rock stars. Maybe nobody wants to be Woody Allen, often a "writer" onscreen. Maybe nobody wants to be as good a reader of stone tablets as Moses, played by Charlton Heston, and certainly nobody wants to be his ghost writer, the Invisible Author on Mount Sinai who published commandments, probably in English.[2] But the subliminal effect of these images is idolatry.

Let's climb to higher elevations. I have in mind three great writers, a Russian, a Ukrainian, and a Chilean, to help me put literature on its proper pedestal.

Alexander Solzhenitsyn, a Red Army tank commander and political prisoner in the Gulag after the Second World War, was expelled from the Writers' Union in November 1969 after *The First Circle* appeared in English in 1968. On 8 October 1970 he was awarded the Nobel Prize for Literature. Immediately he was slandered. People who read his works were dismissed from their jobs and expelled from universities. Late in December 1973 the Russian edition of *The Gulag Archipelago* was published in the West. In it Solzhenitsyn once again challenged a totalitarian regime that between 1918 and 1955 had destroyed tens of millions of innocent people. Early in 1974 he was arrested and charged with high treason. He went into exile.

This is what he wrote in 1970 in his Nobel Prize Lecture:

> [Literature] becomes the living memory of the nation. Thus, it preserves and kindles within itself the flame of her spent history, in a form which is safe from defamation and slander. In this way literature, together with language, protects the soul of the nation.[3]

Vasily Semyonovich Grossman was born in 1905 in a Ukrainian town that was home to one of Europe's largest Jewish communities. From 1924 to 1929 he studied chemistry at Moscow State University but soon realized that his true vocation was literature. His early novels led to his admission in 1937 to the prestigious Union of Soviet Writers. During the Second World War he worked as a reporter for the army newspaper Red Star, covering nearly all the most important battles, including Stalingrad where a million or more soldiers lost their lives. *A Writer at War: A Soviet Journalist with the Red Army, 1941-1945*, available in an English translation in 2005, formed the basis for an even greater book, his novel *Life and Fate*.[4] As Grossman became deeply critical of the Soviet regime, he might have been arrested at any time. Had it not been for Stalin's death in March 1953 just as a new purge against Jews was about to begin, he would have almost certainly perished in the Gulag. He completed *Life and Fate* in 1960. In February 1961 three KGB officers came to Grossman's flat and confiscated the manuscript of the novel and any other relevant material, even carbon paper and typing ribbons. The KGB, however, failed to discover that Grossman, who died in 1964, had made copies of his novel and left them with friends. Twenty years after he completed the novel it was smuggled out of the Soviet Union on microfilm and published to wide acclaim in the West, in France in 1980, in England and the United States in 1985.

Vasily Grossman's place in the history of world literature is assured by *Life and Fate*. It, arguably, is to be rated more highly than Boris Pasternak's *Doctor Zhivago* and Solzhenitsyn's *The First Circle*. The epic breadth and depth of *Life and Fate* offer us a truly powerful understanding of human freedom precisely because all the destinies of the characters are occluded, that is to say, freedom taken totally away illuminates its transcendent glory.

Pablo Neruda, born in Chile in 1904, has been called by Gabriel García Márquez "the greatest poet of the twentieth century—in any language."[5] Chile is a Latin American country where the proposition that literature protects the soul of a nation is deeply felt among its population of seventeen millions. Neruda first became known for his heart-wrenching love poems. When he joined the anti-fascist movement in Spain during the Spanish Civil War, his poetry merged with his political activity. He served the Chilean senate from 1945 until he was exiled for his support for striking miners. He returned to Chile in 1952 and for the next twenty-one years lived there as the people's poet. In 1971 he was awarded the Nobel Prize for Literature. On 11 September 1973 General Pinochet overthrew the popular government. Neruda died of cancer just twelve days later at the age of sixty-nine. Let us listen to his heart's song:

> *I am nothing more than a poet: I love all of you,*
> *I wander about the world I love;*
> *in my country they gaol miners*
> *and soldiers give orders to judges.*
> *But I love even the roots*
> *in my small cold country,*
> *if I had to die a thousand times over*
> *it is there I would die,*
> *if I had to be born...*
> *near the tall wild pines*
> *the tempestuous south wind*
> *the newly purchased bells.*
> *Let none think of me.*
> *Let us think of the entire earth*
> *and pound the table with love....*
> *I did not come to solve anything*
> *I came here to sing*
> *and for you to sing with me.*[6]

Neruda's wake was held in the middle of a muddy, flooded room that was once his library. Books and documents were floating in the mud along with furniture. The day before, a stream had been diverted into the house by the military who smashed everything in sight with their rifle butts and left the house flooded. When the funeral procession began, word spread, and the name of Pablo Neruda opened doors and windows, stopped buses and emptied them, brought people out running from distant streets, thousands of people, almost all poor, people of the shantytowns, all of them becoming in solidarity "Pablo Neruda," each of them singing with him. Suddenly a poor woman had begun to chant Neruda's verses, and everyone had taken up the song: "I have been reborn many times, from the depths/of defeated stars . . . reconstructing the threats/of eternities that I populated with my hands'."[7]

Nearly two decades later, Chile's democratically elected President ordered Neruda's exhumation and reburial on the coast at Isla Negra. Thousands lined the roads and tossed flowers on the poet's flag-draped casket as it passed. The entire nation listened to non-stop radio and television broadcasts devoted to celebration of a poet as, quote, "a national hero, a hero of letters, a hero of humanity."[8] On 12 July 2004 Chile commemorated the centennial of Neruda's birth. Cities and towns held parades. Passing ships sounded their horns. Dignitaries from all over the world gathered at Isla Negra and at Parral, the poet's birthplace. Poetry, it is said, fell from the sky.

It seems pointless to ask why Solzhenitsyn, Grossman, and Neruda wrote. *Compassion and stories and poems are and always have been holding us together. The literary imagination's natural bent toward empathy might actually save us from global annihilation.*

If we think of a book of stories that help to hold humanity together, the King James Bible comes readily to mind. It is a central masterpiece of English literature, for its common readers a single, comprehensive text, for millions, in some sense, divine. Few readers reflect that translators of the KJB possessed the gift of literary authority. The truth is quite startling, as revealed in the following quote from Harold Bloom:

> And yet the King James Bible is itself a composite work, weaving together an allusive web out of the previous translations: not only that of the greatest English translator, William Tyndale, but those of Miles Coverdale and the group that produced the Geneva . . . were absorbed and transmuted by the more than fifty King James translators . . . [9]

In other words, that fountainhead of the English Bible was William Tyndale. His rugged prose is quite possibly the most widely read written English in the world, over the centuries reaching billions of people. Yet few know his name. For undertaking to translate the Bible into English the reformer in October 1536 was strangled and burned.

So, I think we can say that a writer's compulsion or drive or passion to write is an ineluctable fire within. For those in peril—targeted for extermination by dictators and ideologists, for instance—a literary vocation still cannot be avoided. It is a requirement. *The true artist in literature is required to discover and reveal real life as if it were a law of nature.*

Literature is life in the biological sense because we have imagination and memory. Imagination gathers images from memory and makes them available for consciousness. Imagination can be suppressed in favor of reason, but it cannot be eradicated. Samuel Beckett said:

IMAGINATION DEAD IMAGINE[10]

Marcel Proust said outright that real life is literature, said it in the final volume of *In Search of Lost Time*, the longest novel ever written:

> Gradually, thanks to its preservation by our memory, the chain of all those inaccurate expressions in which there survives nothing of what we have really experienced comes to constitute for us our thought, our life, our "reality," and that this life is all that can be reproduced by the art that styles itself "true to life," an art that is as simple as life, without beauty, a mere vain and tedious duplication of what our eyes see and our intellect records, so vain and tedious that one wonders where the writer who devotes himself to it can have found the joyous and impulsive spark that was capable of setting him in motion and making him advance to his task. The greatness, on the other hand, of true art . . . lay, I had come to see, elsewhere: we have to rediscover, to re-apprehend, to make ourselves fully aware of that reality, remote from our daily preoccupations, from which we separate ourselves by an ever greater gulf as the conventional knowledge which we substitute for it grows thicker and more impermeable, that reality which it is very easy for us to die without ever having known and which is, quite simply, our life. Real life, life at last laid bare and illuminated—the only life in consequence which can be said

to be really lived—is literature, and life thus defined is in a sense all the time immanent in ordinary men no less than in the artist. But most men do not see it because they do not seek to shed light upon it.[11]

Given that real life in the Proustian sense is literature, a writer's responsibility for his freedom is to write, to write well, to write, if necessary, in defiance of puritans who hate cakes and ale and of tyrants who hate thought, to write to serve people, not to impress them, and to write so well that once in a while he writes a line or a sentence that's good, if not as good as one of Chaucer's.

And I think that's why Melville, in my opinion our greatest American writer, found reward in writing itself in spite of the world's rejection of him after a notorious debut. At the height of his powers Melville in 1851 bequeathed to us *Moby-Dick*. He died in 1891, forty years after its publication, at which time he had sold a grand total of 3,715 copies. His *Typee*, a Gauguinesque idyll about Polynesian girls, had satisfied book buyers, but *Moby-Dick* outraged them. What could have possessed that mildly salacious sailor to abandon naked women for a whale? During his lifetime, total royalties for all of Melville's books amounted to $5,900 in the United States and $4,500 in England. Then in 1921, thirty years after his death, a biography appeared, Raymond M. Weaver's *Herman Melville: Mariner and Mystic*. By 1957 Newton Arvin was comfortably claiming that the kind of life Melville was raising to the fictive level in *Moby-Dick* was "a life in some of its aspects reminiscent of that led by the Achaean peoples in the days of their folk-wanderings."[12] "What a reader feels in the spacious narrative movement of *Moby-Dick*," Arvin continued, "is not unlike what he feels in the narrative movement of *The Iliad or The Odyssey*."[13] We're way out now, an American novel favorably compared with the greatest of epics from antiquity! In 2011 Nathaniel Philbrick declared that *Moby-Dick* is "nothing less than the genetic code of America"[14] and "the one book that deserves to be called our American bible."[15]

Writers today, whatever their vicissitudes and impediments to happiness, should come in out of silence. Literature forms a great tradition and has gone global. To make the point, here's a short list of novelists and novels to be influenced and inspired by, an arbitrary list based on my desire to re-read them:

Anonymous. *Lazarillo de Tormes*
Miguel de Cervantes. *Don Quixote*
Jane Austen. *Emma*
Charles Dickens. *David Copperfield, Great Expectations*
George Eliot. *Middlemarch*
Nathaniel Hawthorne. T*he Scarlet Letter*
Herman Melville. *Moby-Dick, Billy Budd*
Gustave Flaubert. *Madame Bovary*
Mark Twain. *Huckleberry Finn*
Henry James. *Portrait of a Lady, The Ambassadors*
Fyodor Dostoevsky. *Crime and Punishment, The Brothers Karamazov*
Leo Tolstoy. *War and Peace, Anna Karenina*
Joseph Conrad. *Heart of Darkness, Nostromo*
Marcel Proust. *In Search of Lost Time*
James Joyce. *A Portrait of the Artist as a Young Man*
Joyce Cary. *The Horse's Mout*h
Virginia Woolf. *Mrs. Dalloway*
William Faulkner. *The Sound and the Fury, Go Down, Moses*
John Steinbeck. *The Grapes of Wrath, East of Eden*
Frank Waters. *The Man Who Killed the Deer,*
     The Woman at Otowi Crossing
James Welch. *Fools Crow*
Patrick White. *Voss*
Malcolm Lowry. *Under the Volcano*
Richard Llewellyn. *How Green Was My Valley*
Ralph Ellison. *Invisible Man*
William Styron. *Lie Down in Darkness*
Boris Pasternak. *Dr. Zhivago*
Wallace Stegner. *Angle of Repose*
John Wain. *A Winter in the Hills*
Vasily Grossman. *Life and Fate*
Gabriel García Márquez. *One Hundred Years of Solitude,*
     Love in the Time of Cholera
Toni Morrison. *Beloved*

The modern novel has been around for almost 500 years. *Lazarillo de Tormes*, arguably the first modern novel, was published in 1554 and possibly written as early as 1525.[16] *The Woman at Otowi Crossing*, arguably so visionary it's a twenty-first-century novel, was published in revised form in 1987.[17] Admittedly, my short list, which omits short-story writers, only hints that novels are appearing everywhere. Novelists from Spain, France, England, Wales, Ireland, Australia, Canada, Russia and the United States appear in my list. Among North Americans, Ellison and Morrison are African Americans, Welch is Native American (Blackfeet). There are today, though unlisted, novelists in the Near East and the Far East and Africa.

Another attractive feature of literature, especially in imaginative forms of poetry, fiction, and drama, is its interdisciplinary nature, notably in the past hundred years. Long associated with history, geography, philosophy and psychology, literature is now recognized as a conflation with tens of thousands of years of mythology, *which is essentially imaginative poetry*; it's a cathedral buttressed with evidence from archaeology, anthropology, depth psychology and the so-called "higher criticism" of world religions. Mythology as a source of awe and wonder, not in the sky but in the individual, is reliable human knowledge. Once upon a time mythology was relegated to the nursery so that innocent children could enjoy tales of a god who turns himself into a swan in order to rape a mortal girl. Not anymore.

I've been talking about motives for a vocation in literature. Now I'd like to challenge general motives with serious imperatives for those with the fire within.

The first imperative is to find your true vocation in literature and devote yourself to it. Dylan Thomas loved just the words of nursery rhymes, what they stood for and meant being of very secondary importance. After he began to read for himself, he explained, "love and terror and pity and pain and wonder and all the other vague abstractions that make our ephemeral lives dangerous, great, and bearable" came to life. "And as I read more and more, my love for the real life of words increased until I knew that I must live with and in them, always. I knew, in fact, that I must be a writer of words, and nothing else."[18]

From Dylan Thomas to John Steinbeck is but a short inspirational commuter trip for aspiring writers on the fast train to yesterday. I was teaching fourth-graders at a boys' school in New York when I met Gwyn Steinbeck,

John's second wife, once a radio and band singer and his partner since the filming in Hollywood of *The Grapes of Wrath*. Their second son, John IV, was one of my pupils. I was planning to drive in my Ford to California for a summer vacation and soon I had three passengers, an old schoolmaster from England, Gwyn, and another lady. We were friends on a tour, Gwyn having promised us the Southwest as her John had written about it in *The Grapes of Wrath*. We actually travelled on old Route 66, suffered through the infernal heat of the Mojave Desert, and saw migrant workers policed in orange groves.

While we were waiting in Needles, California, for the temperature to drop at midnight below nuclear-bomb degrees Fahrenheit, Gwyn told me a story. It went like this. John Steinbeck's father was a rancher with a rigid personality who had raised his son to inherit the farm. John, however, had hankered to be a writer ever since he was a boy. When he told his father of his compulsion, his father, figuring he had an inside track, made a deal: John could have two years to succeed as a writer, after which time he had to return to the farm with his tongue hanging out like a hound dog's in a fox hunt. John went around town collecting waste he could use to write on, finding in garbage cans wrapping paper, used envelopes, and discarded billets-doux. Next, he went and holed up in the high Sierras in a cabin and wrote four novels in the two years. He sold one of them in the nick of time and never returned to work on the farm.

I didn't forget Gwyn's story, brief but vivid, a sort of parable about a patriarch and his stubborn son. Since, however, reading Jackson J. Benson's *The True Adventures of John Steinbeck, Writer*, a 1,116-page biography published in 1984, her version of John's apprenticeship seems spotty at best. First of all, his father worked all his life in the respectable society of Salinas, California. He was never a rancher. Moreover, there is no evidence that he had his son on a leash. When John chose to isolate himself in the mountains at Lake Tahoe, his father, in fact, gave him financial support. Second, while it's true that John worked on various manuscripts during his years in Tahoe, the novel he published in 1929, *Cup of Gold*, was not a success. The first of his novels to earn him a measure of fame was *Tortilla Flat*, published in 1935. Third, though, the bit about salvaging paper from garbage cans may be true. John did write on anything available—his father's business papers, pages torn from a ledger, hotel stationary purloined on trips. It could well be, to sum up, that the story Gwyn told me was not of her warping. John delighted in making up fictions about himself.

What is incontestable about Steinbeck's apprenticeship is his persistence as a writer, one that will define the whole of his life, a force that will lead him to greatness. He simply loved to write. Addicted to writing, he serves as a model of the writer who, though isolated and, as it were, defeated by society, in particular by middle-class propriety, prevails through the single-mindedness of his desire. Benson goes to the heart of the matter:

> But what was it in Steinbeck that wouldn't let him stop writing no matter what happened? Perhaps it was the Victorian energy, the high standards of personal success, which, regardless of a conscious rejection, stayed with him as an inheritance from his parents. Perhaps, at the same time, his rebellion drove him to his work... a kind of rage to establish his own identity. Whatever the deep-seated causes may have been, the result was an unreasoning, vague, emotional conviction that all joy and love were somehow inevitably tied up with his writing, and that whatever was beautiful or sublime or worthwhile in his life could only be obtained, not as a product of his work—fame and fortune—but through the process of writing itself.[19]

The second imperative is to tell the truth. From examples I've given of what happened to writers who told the truth in the Soviet regime, it's clear that telling the political truth can get you torture and death. It's as if you're an alternative government. Usually, truth in literature means truth to the human heart. That can be dangerous, too. Tyranny has no heart, no poetry.

Faulkner called this truth "verities of the human heart." When I was at the University of Virginia in the late 1950s, Faulkner came to Charlottesville and met with students. I recall his coming to one such meeting attired in a white Palm Beach suit and gazing unblinkingly around the room like a figure on Mount Rushmore. He spoke in a low, slow Mississippian drawl, for instance pronouncing the word "dilemma" as "dee-leem-uh." When a student asked him about what she called "virtue" in his writing, he replied after a pause:

> Well, let's use a little better word to me than virtue – they're the verities of the human heart. They are courage, pride, compassion, pity. That they are not virtue, or one doesn't try to practice them, in my opinion, simply because they are good. One practices – tries

to practice them simply because they are the edifice on which the whole history of man has [been] founded and by means of which his—as a race he has endured this long. That without those verities he would have vanished.[20]

The third imperative is to create a living world. On the level of human understanding, Shakespeare has probably never been matched. Even topical events which engaged his attention and furnished his plots still repeat themselves at a lower level. On this subject I recommend John Wain's *The Living World of Shakespeare* and Harold Bloom's *Shakespeare: The Invention of the Human.*[21] Joseph Conrad is another example of a great writer who creates a living world. On 31 May 1902, four years after publishing *Heart of Darkness* in *Blackwood's Magazine* and being politely chastised by William Blackwood for its financial failure, Conrad wrote the publisher a letter in which he defended his character and creed. "My work," he wrote,

> shall not be an utter failure because it has the solid basis of a definite intention—first: and next because it is not an endless analysis of affected sentiments but in its essence it is action . . . nothing but action—action observed, felt and interpreted with an absolute truth to my sensations (which are the basis of art in literature)—action of human beings that will bleed to a prick, and are moving to a visible world.[22]

The fourth imperative is to have something to say.

Since we live in a time when we are inundated by waves of shallow, obscure, and mendacious writing in the media, it seems un-American to suggest that there may actually be something worth saying, something critical to human survival. Having something to say implies breadth and depth and vision and passion and heart and courage and grace in some degree or another.

Listen to this scathing passage from Grossman's *Life and Fate*:

> The hide was being flayed off the still living body of the Revolution so that a new age could slip into it; as for the red, bloody meat, the steaming innards—they were being thrown onto the scrapheap. The new age needed only the hide of the Revolution—and this was being flayed off people who were still alive. Those who then slipped into it spoke the language of the Revolution and mimicked its gestures, but their brains, lungs, livers and eyes were utterly different.[23]

Frank Waters, often called "grandfather of Southwestern literature" and sometimes regarded as our "best-known *un*known author," is arguably the greatest writer the American West has ever produced. Both a novelist and a philosopher, if he were judged alongside his contemporaries, Hemingway, Steinbeck, and Faulkner, he wouldn't be found wanting. He died in 1995 at his home in Taos, New Mexico, after a twenty-seven-book career. Presumably because he was a visionary and a Westerner with some Native American ancestry, the cultural establishment tries to deny his existence in spite of numerous nominations of him for the Nobel Prize in Literature. Various 4,000-page megaanthologies of American Literature don't even mention his name. How true indeed that "a Prophet is not without honor, save in his own country!" (Matt. 13:57). Nevertheless, the world will inevitably catch up with what Waters had to say about the future of humankind. He proposed as the evolutionary sanctuary for our psychic life a new world of consciousness, a proposal aimed at curing our spiritual condition rather than at merely expressing it as his contemporaries did. The fragmented wasteland of the modern age, he realized, called for a redemptive vision.

Here is the way Waters describes Maria del Valle, protagonist of his novel, *People of the Valley*, as she lies dying:

> A faint candle-lit darkness, and on the floor the shrouded shape of an old woman with gleaming spectacles of square gold. Like eyes of gold whose value could never be diminished by change, which could never be blinded by age and evil, or corroded by weather and misfortune. Steadily gleaming eyes that burned through time with a faith which could not be dammed, and with a gaze which saw neither the darkness of the day nor the brightness of the morrow, but behind these illusions the enduring reality that makes of one sunset a prelude to a sunrise brighter still.[24]

I conclude this orientation in and introduction to a literary vocation with a summary in three phases—mystery, mission, and meeting.

The mystery of imagination lies in the fact that something is being given and then nourished into being. *The creative work happens to its creator as much as the work is being created by him.* In "A Defense of Poetry," Percy Bysshe Shelley expressed the matter of mystery succinctly:

> A man cannot say, "I will compose poetry." The greatest poet even cannot say it, for the mind in creation is as a fading coal, which

some invisible influence, like an inconstant wind, awakens to transitory brightness.[25]

Joyce's *A Portrait of the Artist as a Young Man*, written almost exactly one hundred years ago, has probably never been equaled for its dramatization of an artist's impulse to fly by way of art from the communal order of so-called "belief" to the largest human view. Here are crucial passages from the point of view of Joyce's protagonist, Stephen Dedalus:

> I will not serve that in which I no longer believe, whether it call itself my home, my fatherland, or my church: and I will try to express myself in some mode of life or art as freely as I can and as wholly as I can, using for my defense the only arms I allow myself to use—silence, exile, and cunning.[26]

> Welcome, O life! I go to encounter for the millionth time the reality of experience and to forge in the smithy of my soul the uncreated conscience of my race.[27]

I think by the word "conscience" Joyce may also have had in mind a cognate word, "consciousness." I'll assume he did. In our time, as I've noted about Waters, we are beginning to grasp the concept of a new world of consciousness, a new mind, an increased awareness. To create the uncreated becomes a mission once the mind is awakened by Shelley's "transitory brightness."

To meet other minds, to convey or transmit to them the sacred unity of life – scientific interconnectedness in quantum physics – is the ultimate phase. A literary vocation is pursued with others in mind. Whether we realize it or not we need literature to hold us together. We meet together because the literature of the ages is already conveyed to us in words from the beginning of our lives. The poets, a generic term including dramatists and fiction writers, come here to sing, and, as Neruda declared, they come here for us to sing with them with our own shared sensibility and creative power. Whether we realize it or not, we've been doing that from the time we first heard songs and then read them; whether we realize it or not, the spiritual oneness of all poetic souls protect us from empathy-exterminators. We are Homer, Aeschylus, Sophocles, Saint Paul, Virgil, Dante, Cervantes, Shakespeare, John Milton, Whitman, Melville and Waters and Edna St. Vincent Millay and so many more writers. They and we are as one. This was Tolstoy's basic tenet, placed in italics in the fifth section of *What Is Art?*

Art is that human activity which consists in one man's consciously conveying to others, by certain external signs, the feelings he has experienced, and in others being infected by those feelings and also experiencing them.[28]

The poets and writers having been called to their task, often at the risk of isolation, banishment, and even death, they sing of our common humanity and Earth, our common home. The poets who really matter to us arouse us with compassion to our own creative enlargement.

Let us go forth with a sense of new and authentic beginnings and a faith that life is not chaos but cosmos. Let us go forth and sing with the poets in return for their songs.

During a short interview with Faulkner, I confessed to him that I wanted to write.

He swiveled around in his chair, took a deceptively professorial pipe from his mouth, looked at me steadily and said softly, "If you have it to do."

I did, and I wanted to be a good writer. Steinbeck said in *Journal of a Novel*, "A good writer always works at the impossible."[29]

If we didn't believe that imagination in general and the literary imagination in particular hold us together and are central to human survival, I would not hesitate to omit from these reflections most of the personal notes that resemble a memoir, but a testimonial of sorts is unavoidable. I found the fire within myself, so why not to tell others of this power within themselves, this prophetic soul?

II

CHAPTER 2

The Used Teabag Man

As soon as the war in Korea ended in 1953, the Army bestowed upon me an honorable discharge and $200. Half of it was gone by the time I reached New York and the apartment of another veteran. He allowed me to stay temporarily rent-free, but I had insisted on paying for rations. Accordingly, I was within a few weeks dining on a diet of rice and caffeine-rich tea from used teabags. I was getting myself ready to take a creative writing course. Before succumbing to necessity and taking a "real" job, I hoped to write at least one short story and test my ability and will to follow my longed-for vocation. I also wanted, after a mind-altering experience of military life, to find my way back to humanity by reading and absorbing works of great literature.

I was reading *Gilgamesh* the day I met The Used Teabag Man. *Gilgamesh*, to the best of my knowledge, is 5,000 years old. It tells of a king of the important Sumerian city-state of Uruk during the Second Early Dynastic Period (2,700-2,500 B.C.). Fragments of the epic have been found which reach back to the time of the earliest writings in any language yet deciphered—not much later than the invention of true writing itself (about 3,000 B.C.). I was finding the story relevant to my own sense of mortality. I hadn't seen combat overseas, but during training I did have a live fragmentation hand grenade carelessly dropped at my feet by a recruit, meaning I had four seconds to live unless I could pick up and throw away the nuisance. A friend of mine in Officer Candidate School, who had machine-gunned charging Chinese troops in Korea, had been killed by machine-gun fire during a training exercise on an infiltration range. So, yes, *Gilgamesh* seemed, in a way, my story. That king was crushed to learn that he must live in a hostile environment, threatened by death, knowing the pain of loss, yet having a mind able to triumph over mortality through harmony of memory and imagination.[30]

One afternoon, feeling light-headed from lack of nourishment, I decided to take a walk. The weather was cold with a threat of Christmas. Contrary to what one might expect from circumstances I've described, I was also feeling exhilarated. Thanks to my love of literature in general and discovery of *Gilgamesh* in particular my mere mortal years—twenty-four of them—had, because we can live vicariously through stories, a life span of 5,000 years!

I strolled some fifty blocks up Broadway and stopped in the vicinity of 125th Street where I spotted a small diner. It would cost me a precious nickel, but if I half-filled my cup of coffee with sugar, I could fuel my return to the apartment and to my vicarious residence in ancient Sumeria. Customers were leaving the diner as I entered it. I was the only person in the place except for the counterman, a bald-headed black man who studied me quizzically as if I might be a Section Eight vet with a stick-up gun. I couldn't blame him for the eyeballs in his head. My officer's "pink" trousers were frayed at the kneecaps, my Ike jacket had no ribbons. My unpolished boots with worn-down heels should have been turned in the direction of the nearest church.

I sat on a stool, pulled out a forlorn nickel, and plopped it on the counter, whereupon the counterman asked me with a smile what I'd like. I told him. He served me the coffee, and I thanked him. We seemed to have reached an understanding that I wasn't Hitler's best friend. I reached for the container for sugar, poured about ten tablespoonfuls into the cup, and was soon sipping a polluted liquid presumably bottled from the Tigris and Euphrates rivers.

The counterman was nervously consulting his wristwatch, jerking his head about to study the street through the condensed fog on his window. I reckoned he was expecting a V.I.P.'s arrival. Suddenly busying himself as if he'd identified his celebrity, he set a place on the counter in front of the stool next to mine—knife, fork, spoon, plate, cup, saucer. He put the containers of sugar and cream close to those items and went and fetched a globe full of hot water.

A bent-over, Bronze Age man, feet wrapped in burlap sacks, stumbled through the door, letting in a blast of frigid air. Ruffled by what was becoming a gale-force wind, his long white hair flowed behind him like a scarf of snow.

With the exception of Salvation Army spectacles, his features bore resemblance to an iguana's, the raisin-wrinkly skin so old and weathered that I wondered whether he had a home and someone to look after him east of Eden. He had to be chilled to the bone. He wasn't wearing under his tattered Joseph's coat any more protective clothing than I was. Perhaps it was a hand-me-down from Abraham. Perhaps Abraham had inherited it from someone who could trace it to the author of *Gilgamesh*. Perhaps the old man *was* the author of *Gilgamesh*! He personified Imagination. I was dizzy in the head all right.

He shuffled his way to the stool next to mine, to the place set for him as if he were that king. As he sat down, he opened his mouth wide and groaned. His Stonehenge of teeth was sad to behold. The scent of his breath was as if the lid of a sarcophagus excavated from the Sphinx had suddenly been lifted.

The counterman came and filled the sovereign ghost's cup with hot water. As Imagination he deserved the deference the counterman was showing.

From a pocket inside his coat Imagination removed two items, a rolled-up newspaper and a teabag damp as a Lilliputian's diaper. He dipped the bag into the cup of hot holy water and left it there until the water's color turned as golden yellow as a Byzantine halo, fit for a saint. Clutching the sugar container, he poured enough of that power supply to, like poetry, light up drear Manhattan like a Christmas tree. After slurping his tea, he unfolded the newspaper, removed from it half a gnawed eel, put it on his plate, and, using the knife and fork, speared, chewed, and swallowed pieces of it, if "chewed" is the right word for what passed through, like a golf ball, his apple of Adam. After a while, Imagination wordlessly and without paying a nickel heaved himself to his feet and, with wandering steps and slow, through Eden took his solitary way.

I wanted to blame parents, K-through-12, four years of college, almost three years of the military and now a bit of hardscrabble reality for delays in my development. Although I recognized literature as my true vocation, I was afraid to devote myself to it. Of course, I was grateful for all the experiences granted to me, for all the little acts, remembered and unremembered, of kindness and of love, for the mean and dangerous ones, too, but to the extent that my life seemed *un*lived, I felt miserable. Why had I chosen a literary vocation? Why did I fear becoming a Used Teabag Man?

When I was two, I flushed my mother's rubies down the toilet. Deducing from this behavior evidence of incredible talent, Mom spanked me so that I would have something to write about in future. She further contributed to it by reading poetry and fairy tales to me. The art of writing limericks and puppy-love stories she demonstrated for me with the same intensity of concentration I had hitherto experienced when I pressed my nose against windows of candy stores.

As I grew older, I discovered that literary people like my Dad liked arts and whiskey. He took me to Duke University to watch Massine of the Ballet Russe de Monte Carlo dance and to listen to the New York Philharmonic Orchestra.[31] Whiskey transformed morose professors like Dad into social misfits who might at any minute cut a caper in our living room and sing bawdy English songs. My favorite song at his parties, as I hid behind the sofa like an alien from Mars, was the one Dad sang about poor, honest girls who meet bloody bishops, lose their names in vain, and become whores, whatever they were. When Dad's colleagues had finished drinking his bourbon highballs and had been driven home as DUI as proverbial sailors, I pretended to help Mom tidy up the room. Actually, I was looking only for half-empty glasses. As soon as I had some of them to myself in the kitchen, I would chug-a-lug leftover Jack. Then, after we all went upstairs to our beds, I, alone in my room, could sing a wee bit tipsily the music-hall song I had memorized, even though I couldn't do the cockney accent which Dad had learned to imitate when he was at Oxford as a Rhodes Scholar. It went like this:

> It's th' sime the 'ol world over,
> T'is the pore what gits th' blime,
> It's th' rich gits all the grighvy,
> Ain't it all a bloody shime.

By the age of twelve I had switched from leftover whiskey to *Oliver Twist*. Because Charles Dickens seemed to have a good opinion of girls, especially virgins, I believed that they needed writers to keep them from losing their names in vain.

One New Year's Eve my devilishly clever older sister tacked a sprig of myrtle over a doorway just as girls and Artful Dodgers in my seventh-grade class arrived dressed up for a party that Mom had arranged because she believed that writers have to suffer other people to be able to write. We danced to the cloying croons of Bing Crosby and Frank Sinatra. I had to fox-trot with a fat girl from the country-club set. She lured me under the sprig of myrtle. Suddenly she bear-hugged me and masticated my mouth as if I were a double dip of ice cream. I decided there and then to abandon priggishness about protecting girls and, instead, play hooky from school. I had found my vocation. I could read and write forever and not become a whore, myself.

I had talent: I could spot a Wizard of Smug behind his or her curtain of sanctimony. In elementary school there had been at least two of these wizards. One was my geography teacher. She had breasts so pendulous she was supporting them, I imagined, with a sling she had used in another impercipient life to hurl elephant turds at the siege of Troy. I felt sorry about her physical handicap until she started picking on kids from the Mill Village. I didn't cotton to that. We were all one people in The Depression, weren't we? Just because their daddies were slaving away in the hosiery mills for a few dollars a day didn't mean they didn't provide their plumb-wore-out wives with soap and claw-footed bathtubs. Old Smug seemed to believe that these children, whose mothers must have scrubbed them with potassium hydroxide, as well as clothed them in starched linsey-woolsey dresses and dungarees from five-and-dime stores, would have Jesus holding his nose at the Last Judgment. After roll call she made the Mill Village kids stand up for inspection. When she couldn't find dirty fingernails or head lice, she would say sarcastically, "HOORAH for you!" Out in the playground I played baseball with some of the Mill Village boys and shared my Baby Ruth candy bars with them and could tell from the way they lifted lowered eyes that they had been feeling small.

Another Wizard was the Chief of the Durham City Fire Department. Once a year when we at George Watts School were assembled in the playground for Fire Drill, he showed up in uniform and sang for us, the way I remember:

> *Put on the skillet,*
> *Slip on the lid,*
> *Mammy's gonna bake*
> *A l'il short'nin' bread.*
> *Dat ain't all*
> *She gonna do,*
> *Mammy's gonna make*
> *A l'il coffee too.*
> *Mammy's l'il baby loves*
> *Short'nin' short'nin'*
> *Mammy's l'il baby loves*
> *Short'nin' bread.*

We applauded, we were so dumb and white. Somewhere off in "Haiti," kids like us were going to "Colored" schools we seldom heard about. We knew they existed, though. I suspected the Chief of the Durham City Fire Department didn't visit those schools. If he did, he didn't sing in them about Mammies.

With Mom's help I solved the Sex and Education Problem. All she had to do was telephone the secretary to the principal of Junior High School and tell her I was sicker than a grass-eating dog. Mom had been a trained nurse before she married Dad, a frequent patient in hospitals and a voracious reader, all which activities, I reckoned, required beds. Since she wanted me to be a writer, she fancied I should go to bed to write. That was all right with me. I could stay in bed at home and write stories about Andy, our cocker spaniel, a sex-maniac—whenever there was a bitch in heat, he would disappear in the woods for a week—and for Chip Wilson, the six-year-old crippled boy who lived next door. Chip's arms and legs were twisted like pretzels, saliva drooled from his mouth, and he liked my stories so much he made a sound in his throat like a raven's raucous call. I loved Chip. Large was his bounty and his soul, sincere.

As I grew older, I had drilled into my vanity the intolerable curse of family relatives, weird ancestors like George Washington's grandfather and living in-laws like Teddy Roosevelt's physician, Uncle Alexander Lambert, after whom I'd been named by Mom without my consent. Artists and writers were the relatives I most admired. There were two artists on my mother's side in Manchester, Connecticut. Seth Cheney (1810-1856) was one of the earliest American artists in black and white crayon and excelled in giving spirituality to his portraits and ideal female faces.[32] Uncle Russell Cheney (1881-1945) was a master of American Impressionism. The artists stood for what I could only dream of becoming.[33]

It was my father, William Blackburn (1899-1972), who inspired me to take up the scholarly, not so much the creative, side of a literary vocation. Born in a Presbyterian mission in Iran and raised in small Bible-Belted South Carolina towns, he had needed truth and shoes. His grandmother, once treasurer of the Confederacy, provided shoes. Truth he found by challenging dogma in his thinking and teaching. Because he had a sense of irreverence, he was indisposed to read the Bible as other than literature in English, and so he refused to become a minister as his parents wanted him to be. He would read to his uptight students the bit about Gulliver's pissing on a fire on the island of the Lilliputians. He was obviously beloved by his students, back in the days of euphemisms. He taught English at Duke and, after 1932, a course he called

"Literary Composition." In those days a course in "Creative Writing" was considered anathema by professors trained to swat up "facts" in the history of literature. If you were a "poet," you could not be a "scholar," even though poetry was the subject matter for "research." For years my once-upon-a-time-starved father feared that he might lose his job if he let it be known that he was teaching, at students' request, "creative writing." Even today, sadly, oft-published imaginative writers and their mentors are sometimes regarded as beneath the academic salt.

According to those who knew him best, Dad had, himself, the makings of an originative novelist. He chose instead to teach writers, also to edit them. Wont to say to me that he "turned out good students," I can look back and understand he was referring to William Styron (Pulitzer Prize, Fiction), Mac Hyman (*No Time for Sergeants*), Fred Chappell (Bollinger Prize, Poetry), Reynolds Price (National Book Critics Circle Award), William deBuys (finalist, Pulitzer Prize, Nonfiction) and Anne Tyler (Pulitzer Prize, Fiction).[34] Perhaps because he had forced himself to become a "scholar" only—he always told me he lacked "confidence" (a feeling of inadequacy I shared)—he was a nervous wreck, my dad, especially in his later years when he was still writing letters with nib pen and ink, his handwriting looking like King Lear's. His critical acumen, though, had, according to testimony from those students, been combined with charisma to make him a greathearted teacher. When he read an early draft of my first novel, I expected him to condemn it with an expression on his face of hypnotic horror. To my amazement he told me it was "strong." Years after his death I discovered in his correspondence with William Styron that he considered *Lie Down in Darkness* "strong." I wouldn't try to compare myself with Styron, but, perhaps, Dad had been encouraging me after all.

In order to make the point about an unlived life, I have to resort to belittling some of the lucky and wonderful things that happened to me between 1944 and 1965. How could I blame my parents for loving me so much they had raised me with the wings of Icarus, expecting me to fly but not to fly too high?

> 1944-47, won a scholarship to attend Phillips Academy, Andover, Massachusetts. Published a sketch in the school magazine

> 1947-51, won a scholarship to attend Yale University, graduated B.A. in English, minor in Philosophy

1951-53, volunteered as a private, U.S. Army during the Korean War, commissioned lieutenant out of Officer Candidate School

1953-54, seminar in creative writing, The New School, New York, published in 1956 the story I wrote there

1954-55, attended on the G.I. Bill The University of North Carolina at Chapel Hill. Graduated M.A. in English, minor in French. Published a poem. Wrote a thesis on Gustave Flaubert and Henry James

1955-56, taught fourth-graders at the Allen-Stevenson School, New York

1956-57, taught eighth- and ninth-graders at the American School in London. Married Jane Allison of Filey, Yorkshire

1957-1959, Fellow in American Literature, The University of Virginia. Birth of David Blackburn. Published a short story and a poem, won a First Prize from the Academy of American Poets

1959-60, attended Cambridge University and studied under Dr. David Daiches the origins of the modern novel. Published a poem

1960-61, Instructor in English, Hampden-Sydney College, Virginia

1961-63, Cambridge University. Graduated Ph.D. Degree in English. Birth of Philip Blackburn. Wrote dissertation on the history of the picaresque novel, 1554-1954, in Spain, France, England, Germany and the United States

1963-65, Instructor in English and Creative Writing, The University of Pennsylvania, Philadelphia.

The biblical life span is three-score years and ten. At the age of thirty-five in 1965, I was, as they say in the Deep South, in tall cotton: graduate of respectable schools, professor in the Ivy League.

Luckily, the fire within just wouldn't go out even though I had barely banked hot ashes with the tightly packed fuel of little promise.

Until Robert Penn Warren arrived on the scene Yale had apparently offered no courses in what has become known as "creative writing." One day the

English Department announced that "Red" Warren would lead qualified students in a workshop of the kind. Rushing over to the department, I was first to place my name on a list of prospective students for the course. Back in the dorm I read *All the King's Men* (1946), Warren's powerful novel, and waited for the announcement that my soul was saved in the Blood of the Bulldog. A few days later I received a note to the effect that I had been disqualified. Why? My academic record showed I had flunked Chemistry. *Chemistry?* Imaginative writers need Chemistry? Was Warren writing the last word on poison gas, atomic bombs, plastic jock straps and deodorants for pet skunks?

I spent the summer of 1950 in Seattle and got a job at a marina on Lake Washington putting gas in expensive motorboats. I met an old sourdough, author of *A Logger's Odyssey*, "chloroform in print," Mark Twain might have said of it, and he invited me to the Seattle Press Club to introduce me to a "Miss Lulu," owner of *The Fairbanks News-Miner* in the Territory of Alaska. She was looking to hire a reporter, while I was looking for a way to drop out of Yale. Needing an antidote to the chemistry of oligarchy, I accepted the invitation. As a reporter in Alaska I could write up breaking news about grizzlies.

Her full name was Lulu Fairbanks of Fairbanks, Alaska. To impress her with my business smarts, I said I would think it over and call her in the morning. Next morning, I saw a newspaper headline that declared that North Korea had invaded South Korea. I decided to go back to Yale, graduate, and postpone discovery of the missing 99% of Americans, the ones I needed to write about someday.

My senior year, Bill Styron invited me to come down from New Haven for a party in Greenwich Village. I hurried on down. At his apartment on the West Side he showed me final chapters of *Lie Down in Darkness* as they were neatly written out with #2 pencil on yellow legal sheets. He placed Handel's *Messiah* on a record player. I then and there became a novelist. All you needed to be a novelist, I figured, was to take a writing workshop at the New School, as Bill had done, buy lots of legal-sized paper and #2 pencils, play the *Messiah*, and drink martinis with the intelligentsia in Greenwich Village. I was on my way.

The way that was soon to be my way was, instead, "R.A. all the way," Regular Army, private, U.S. Army Signal Corps, in the pressure-cooker heat of Georgia. As an English major from Yale, I was regarded by my superiors as uniquely qualified to teach recruits how to throw hand grenades and stick bayonets into straw dummies. I did so well as a weapons instructor, I was sent to Yucca Flat in Nevada to be dutifully radiated by an atomic bomb. I experienced a new dimension of history, Virgil's "new order of the ages begins." I had something to write about and did years later in four novels.

I was also getting a writer's experience when I received Special Orders to report to Smokebomb Hill, Fort Bragg, North Carolina, as a psychological warfare officer. My MOS was to supervise the efforts of artists in creating propaganda leaflets to be dropped over Chinese troops in Korea. As soon as we destroyed the enemy's morale in this manner, I could light out for New York and write. My English vocabulary was, however, shrinking. It seemed necessary to communication in the military to use the f-word as a noun, adjective, and verb; if you employed "mother" as a prefix to the f-word and "up" as a suffix, you could qualify for a postwar job as a scriptwriter in Hollywood. If not that, your training in propaganda could lead to a career in advertising, public relations, journalism, politics, organized religion and playing Santa Claus in department stores.

A French Foreign Legionnaire at Fort Bragg gave me photographs he had smuggled out of Indochina. I showed these pictures—Vietnamese widows weeping in ruined villages—to a PsyWar captain acquainted with a little-known war there. He agreed to write an article for me. I had decided, in order to improve my writing and to keep my leaflet boys busy, to found a magazine, *Sight: A Magazine of Psychological Warfare.* Having a lead story with pictures, I printed the first issue and informed the unenlightened brass about Indochina. I sent copies of *Sight* to the C.I.A., Radio Free Europe, and President Eisenhower's Psychological Strategy Board. I took pride in the fact that the men in my Loudspeaker & Leaflet platoon were gung ho to confuse Commies. I was an editor, on my way to be a writer.

My other duty on Smokebomb Hill was to serve as officer of a mess for enlisted men. Having no experience in operating a cafeteria, I thought all I had to do was show up at meal times and satisfy myself about the "eye appeal" of offal. For everything else I relied upon the Mess Sergeant, a 250-pound black man with combat ribbons and the charm of a Satchmo.

One morning a major showed up at company HQ and informed me I was under investigation for court-martial. Anything I said, he said, might be held against me. I said, therefore, nothing about poetry, evolution, women's liberation, or the idea that eating people is wrong. While I was trying to keep my jaw from dropping off its hinges, Major, as I'll call him, was also informing me in a suave manner that he was a Yale man too. The problem, he told me in the tone of an old frat pal, was that "Washington" was having a hisser over the contents of my sweet little magazine.

"Why am I being interrogated, sir?" I asked.

As Mess Officer, he explained, I was responsible for the "head count." If the head count number was greater than the number of meals actually served, someone was ordering more supplies of food than we needed, then selling surplus on the black market in nearby Fayetteville.

"Is that happening in my mess, sir?"

"What can you tell me, Lieutenant?"

He had hit me where it hurt. "Nothing, sir," I lied. The truth was, I'd left responsibility for head counts to the Mess Sergeant.

Major said we'd meet again in a week's time. For someone who was wearing on the shoulders of his rumpled uniform the golden insignia of his rank, this officer seemed an imposter, neither a Yalie nor a soldier. He wore no fruit salad. He returned my salutes with a right-arm motion suitable for throwing a football. As for his being a Yalie, I had to wonder why an alleged representative of the alleged ruling class—to which I felt no allegiance—would make a career in the Army. He probably thought I was the phony one, not he. Members of the Class of 1951 did not volunteer as privates in the Army, did they? To me, the explanation for my lack of ruling-class savoir vivre was simple: I was going to be drafted anyway, I wanted experiences I could write about if I lived to tell tales, and I believed, with respect to any opportunity, in starting at the bottom and working my way up.

The person in charge of food supplies was a Warrant Officer P-----. If he was involved in hijacking supplies, as I suspected, he certainly wouldn't want a dumb second looey putting a spanner in the works.

"Torture tactics," Warrant Officer P----- said after I had gone to his office and explained my situation. "You tell that mother-f-ing spook to call me, Lieutenant. I reckon they's black marketing goin' on. Ain't got nothing to do with you except you stumbled on some classified bull-shit." Indochina was classified in 1953. Imagine.

After thanking the Warrant Officer and turning to leave, I paused and asked him what good would it do for Major to call.

The Warrant Officer sighed and looked me in the eye. "Lieutenant," he said wearily, "it's like this. Your Mess Sergeant is about to retire. Half the time he's been in this man's army he's been in the stockade. I ain't sayin' he's a habitatin' thief, but let's let him retire on a pension, Dear John, all she wrote."

I relayed the Warrant Officer's message to Major, taking care not to reveal to him he was a mother-f-ing spook. He now said I was no longer the subject of investigation. To avoid future court-martial, however, I would have to scuttle the magazine and cease exercising my ambition to understand English sentences.

"No problem, sir," I said, parting with the First Amendment.

That time I met the Used Teabag Man came about in 1953 at Christmastime. After taking employment at an insurance company, I enrolled in that creative writing course at the New School, as Bill Styron had advised me to do. I shared an apartment, as I've mentioned, with a Korean veteran. He wanted to major in bagpipes at Julliard. Since he liked to play them inside the small apartment, I retreated to the bathroom. Sitting on the stool with typewriter on knees, I wrote my first short story, "The Golden River." When I submitted it in the spring of 1954 to John Maloney, Styron's friend and my teacher at the New School, he requested permission to have it published in their trade hardcover. *Jesus, Sir, no problem.*

I had, in fact, problems. Styron had taken Hiram Haydn's novel-writing workshop at the New School, and his career was launched. And Haydn invited me to join that class. But in order to study full-time I would have to quit my job at the insurance company and have, accordingly, no money. I had no love either. My wild Irish girlfriend, an actress named Maria, went on the road as understudy to Veronica Lake, the movie star of peekaboo-hair-style fame. All too aware of the lives of artists, Maria broke off our engagement and my heart so that, I guess, I would have something to write about in future. I had reached a fork in the road. Of course, I realized, I could draw upon the G.I. Bill if I went to graduate school. By going to graduate school I was endangering my identity as an unpublished writer of unwritten novels and committing myself to become an English teacher like Dad. I hated the like-father-like-son syndrome, but I was sure going to die as a Used Teabag Man. The partial solution to the problem was to take the path to a teaching career but to bend that path toward the art of fiction until the two paths could, eventually, converge along parallel lines in the same direction. For a master's degree, I would concentrate study on Henry James's technique, especially that of a center of consciousness, and on Gustave Flaubert's technique, especially that by means of which the artist could be like God in the universe, everywhere present but nowhere seen. With luck I could eventually sneak in the back door to the Used Teabag Man's Bronze Age smithy.

One afternoon in 1955 in Chapel Hill, I looked out the window of my $40-a-month bed-sitter on Henderson Street and spotted a postman stuffing an envelope in my mailbox. I dashed downstairs and retrieved the envelope. It contained galleys of "The Golden River," the forgotten short story, now to be published in *American Vanguard*. That weekend, floating in the sky like a gaseous balloon, I went to Durham and showed the galleys to Dad. "They've placed you *first* in volume," he chortled magisterially. Right there I felt as if I could have been credited with having written an eye-witness account of the Book of Genesis.

Fast-forward to Philadelphia the winter of 1964-1965 . . .

I was beginning to grow wary of being introduced to people with the title Doctor. Once in a while someone with the worst liver complaint since vultures devoured the reproducing ones inside Prometheus would have to be undeceived about the nature of my Ph.D., Doctor of Philosophy, not of Medicine. It entitled me by a stroke of luck to employment as a professor at the University of Pennsylvania. The English Department there put me in charge of Freshman Honors and gave me permission to teach Creative Writing. No one breathed down my neck. I chose my own syllabi. Among my students in Creative Writing were Candice Bergen, soon to decamp to Hollywood and later in her life to become an author, and Stephen Berg, soon to found *The American Poetry Review*. As an adjutant for visiting writers, I was honored to serve as an escort for Archibald MacLeish, Ralph Ellison, May Sarton and Philip Roth. Sad to recall, I was sitting beside MacLeish as he, unabashedly weeping, watched on TV the funeral procession for his friend, President Kennedy. I was on stage with Ellison when he put down a white man's heckling by intoning, "You're not so white yourself!" May Sarton told my class to begin a poem or a story with a strong image. That has been my mantra ever since. I had a wonderful job.

On 17 December 1964, things fell apart.

My mother's only sister, Mrs. Helen Knapp ("Aunt Hen") of Kittery, Maine, and Boston, had as a widow raised two daughters, Emily and Betsy, my first cousins. A homesick boy when I first went to Andover, I had visited Aunt Hen in Maine and discovered that we had a literary bond of sorts. Through the Cheney family and her husband, she had known H. Phelps Putnam, the poet; Uncle Russell Cheney's partner, Professor F.O. Matthiessen ("Matty") of Harvard; and Matty's protégé, Professor Leo Marx of M.I.T. I didn't need to be told that Matthiessen had revolutionized the study of American Literature with his book, *American Renaissance: Art and Expression in the Age of Emerson and Whitman* (1941). Although I didn't read Marx's lament,

The Machine in the Garden: Technology and the Pastoral Ideal (1964), until later, I knew that Aunt Hen had befriended Matty's brilliant students.[35] One further note: while recovering my heart from Maria, whose favorite platitude was "In the midst of life we are in death," I had spent a week at Aunt Hen's cottage in Kittery. A widow who understood loneliness, she encouraged me to write a sonnet about it. After the poem was later published in *The Carolina Quarterly*, I was so satisfied with feeling sorry for myself in public that I never wrote another sonnet. My inner Edith Piaf still loves the word *chagrin*, though.

I had met Cousin Emily twice, once when she was visiting Yale from Vassar College, later at a conference she attended with her husband, Donald Pitkin. When Mrs. Emily Knapp Pitkin, older than I by only a year, died on December 17, 1964, the tragedy changed my life. She had died from complications following the birth of her first child. She had had a serious heart problem. Doctors had warned her of the risk of death were she to bring a child to full term. She took the risk. In the midst of life, she really was in death. She sacrificed her life for the sake of giving birth to life. To devotees of the heroines in the novels of Henry James, she had truly *lived*.

I went to Cambridge, Massachusetts, to attend the memorial service.

Early in their marriage the Pitkins had gone to live in remote Italian villages, the people there "from the Stone Age," Emily had written me in a humorous vein. Don's Italian colleague, Manlio Rossi-Doria, who also attended the service, wrote this eulogy, one translated by Don as "In Memory of Emily Pitkin."

> On the 17th of December 1964, Emily Pitkin died in Cambridge, Mass. There had been born to her a few months before a baby girl, the first child, long desired. A difficult pregnancy had taken all of her strength. Then, happy, in the full of her recovery, she was stricken with an illness such that in a few days it carried her away . . .

> She came for the first time to Italy in 1950, just married to Donald Pitkin, then at the beginning of his career in Anthropology. With him she established immediate ties to our country, and to many of us gave a relationship (*un rapporto*) so direct and intense as to become essential and permanent elements of our lives.
> Choosing Sermoneta as a typical and traditional rural community in which to study the fundamental relationships of a peasant

society, Don and Emily returned to Italy with the possibility of remaining for more than a year. Living within the little town on the slopes of Monti Lepini, above Agro Pontino, and joining in the life there for long months, they came to know not only all the people, every part of the surrounding countryside, but left to many of the inhabitants their affectionate friendship.

The experience of Sermoneta was for Emily of fundamental importance, not so much to change her, but more to render her still more entirely herself. The continuity of relations with those simple yet rich people indeed brought out in her that natural trait of her personality, which she had always carried within her from the time of childhood—still living then in that most refined air of cultural New England—to all the essential things of life, with a human warmth, a profound and direct way, a simplicity that none of us will ever be able to forget. It is not too much to imagine that in some house to which she became attached in Sermoneta there was born in her the decision of becoming a social aid, and that, returning to America, she followed those studies and there dedicated herself to them for the future, and gave a great part of her time.

Speaking of her shortly after her death, during a severe and beautiful religious ceremony in Christ Church of Cambridge, one of her friends, Professor Leo Marx, had noted that "Emily loved Italy, the hot Mediterranean sun and the unguarded, expressive life of the ways of the Italians. The quality that she admired in the Italians was that which seemed to distinguish her from her Yankee heritage. But one can never say that she had repudiated her origins, because at the bottom of her Italian qualities, of her exuberance, of her instinctive life, there was always a solid nucleus of New England rectitude, a kind of elegant discrimination, refined aristocracy, a discrimination not closed in upon itself, but open eagerly outward, to all things of the entire world."

Well said of that which made the felicity that rose from her friendship in which so many of us for years have rejoiced. In her Italian sojourn, in the hospitality of her home in America, in the living contact engendered even when she was far away, of her optimistic enthusiasm for all generous ideals, of her warm participation in that which most profoundly engaged every one of us, a felicity endures in memory and will endure always.[36]

A light snow was falling that afternoon in Cambridge. The church was filled. When we sang Emily's favorite New England hymn, "For Those in Peril on the Sea," it penetrated the thin flesh of all our hearts. Yankees, like stiff-upper-lip Victorians who read the novels of Dickens, wept. Awakened in me was the resolution to live, like Emily, in peril.

After the service, family and friends gathered at the Pitkin home on a quiet street in Cambridge. I sat for a while with Aunt Hen and Betsy. I realized I must resign my position at the university, take the family back to England, where we could at that time live cheaply, and give myself fully to imaginative writing. I went to the bartender and asked for a Scotch on the rocks. I wandered into an empty room and gazed out the window at a gathering blizzard of blowing snow. Yes, I would leave the Ivy League, the Dream of Success, and unused teabags. In my heart I thanked Emily for showing me the way to abandon the unlived life for life in peril on the sea. Her sacrifice gave me the courage to stir the fire within into flame.

I seemed to see out there in the street a 5,000-year-old writer named Imagination. He was leaning into the wind, clutching a tattered coat. Behind him streamed long white hair. Suddenly the Used Teabag Man metamorphosed himself into a callow, rolled-out-thin Carolina boy willing at last to peer into the Abyss, as Gilgamesh had done, and make committed contact with the consciousness of being. For a split second the Used Teabag Man seemed to turn his head and smile at me with a mouth full of miraculously new teeth, my teeth, minus the wisdom ones. I heard *his* words as *my* words on the wind: *Follow meeeeee* . . .

CHAPTER 3

Two Roads Converged

"Two roads diverged in a yellow wood, /And sorry I could not travel both": the opening lines of Robert Frost's poem "The Road Not Taken" are among the best-known in all of American poetry, as are the end lines about taking the road "less traveled by" and how that decision "made all the difference."

The road to a literary vocation is certainly one less traveled by than many others, and the decision to take that road certainly makes the difference in the sense of commitment. The quarrel I have with Frost's poem—it's more of a quibble than a quarrel—is its sly pronunciamiento that one cannot travel two roads at the same time. For me, both my roads, scholarship and writing, were creative, thus conceivably convergent rather than divergent. I'm sure most writers, especially women with a family, struggle for similar balance.

I was forty-six before I finished my first novel and, after rejections of it, fifty when I published it. For years I harbored discontent about myself for not daring to do—for very sensible reasons—what I knew I had to do. When the opportunity to work on a first novel arrived, I took that road, whereupon the sense I had of myself as a traveler divided within himself dissolved into a precarious balance. I was, for better or worse, a poet *and* a scholar. I hoped I was also a socially responsible cog, though infinitesimally small in a wheel large as the universe. The Gauguin-like artist celebrated in W. Somerset Maugham's novel *The Moon and Sixpence* has the fire within. But he abandons not only his successful job as a stockbroker but also his wife and children. He is to me in judgmental moods an insufferable cad. Those who live in an alternative reality admire and forgive such artists, I admit, if they are canonical and misogynistic enough. Written a century ago, "The Road Not Taken" adumbrates for us today a peculiarly American dilemma: how long can the myth of an individual's unbridled liberty continue when it is delusional to deny there is a global demand for cooperation in saving the planet? Unless all roads lead to planetization, there will be no forsaken road left to be sorry about.

In the previous chapter I belittled myself for taking the road of scholarship at the seeming expense of the road of creativity. Now with a backward glance I can plot the convergence of two roads.

1965: Wootton, Boar's Hill, near Oxford, England. Writing full-time

1968: First draft completed of work-in-progress, *The Cold War of Kitty Pentecost*. Part-time professor, University of Maryland, European Division, and part-time lecturer, Oxford Polytechnic University

1972: Death of William Blackburn

1973: Professor of English and Creative Writing (beginning series of promotions) at University of Colorado at Colorado Springs (UCCS). First meeting with Yusef Komunyakaa

1974: Founder and editor-in-chief, *Writers' Forum*. Divorce from Jane Blackburn

1975: Marriage to Inés Henry (née Dölz)

1979: *The Cold War of Kitty Pentecost* (republished in 2016) and *The Myth of the Picaro* (republished in 2014 in UNC Press Enduring Editions)

1982: First meeting with Frank Waters

1987: *The Interior Country*

1991: *A Sunrise Brighter Still*. UCCS Faculty Book Award

1993: *Higher Elevations*

1995: *Suddenly a Mortal Splendor* (republished in 2015). Runner-up,

Colorado Book Award. UCCS Chancellor's Award. Professor emeritus
2001: *Creative Spirit*

2002: Foreword, *Pure Waters*

2004: *Meeting the Professor*

2005: Frank Waters Award

2010: *Gifts from the Heart.* Runner-up, Colorado Book Award

2014: *The Door of the Sad People*

2015: *The Voice of the Children in the Apple Tree*, completing a single quartet of novels on the Virgilian theme, "a new order of the ages begins."

2019: *The Fire Within*

2020: Forthcoming: *The Emergence of Frank Waters: A Critical Reader*, co-edited with John Nizalowski.

The name of Odysseus in *The Odyssey* means that an identity achieved through struggle is painful and also inevitably gives pain.[37] Before, therefore, I extoll the merits of anyone's career as a writer, I think it fair to point out that in terms of relationships it doesn't promise you and others a rose garden, to borrow a phrase made famous by Joanne Greenberg.[38]

Artists need time alone, time without distractions, time to submerge into themselves mentally. While artists are submerging, spouses and visitors, Coleridge's Persons from Porlock,[39] are apt to feel neglected. A kind of *ménage à trois* develops: the writer, the Other, the Typewriter or Computer. John Nichols had this experience and the self-deprecating humor to write about it. His wife Miel, much younger than he, had the temperament of the flamenco dancer she became. He himself is accustomed to writing all night! The author of *The Milagro Beanfield War* explains what happened to their volatile marriage:

> Unfortunately, my wife, Miel, is not exactly a happy camper. She thinks I probably had a lobotomy back in my youthful days.

She feels I throw out too many babies with the bathwater on my maniacal quests for integrity. But I tell her, "Mellow out, relax, stick with me, kid, and even if the roof leaks and the termites undermine our foundations, it won't matter one whit, because as long as we have each other we'll just dance down a delightful yellow brick road without a care in the world into a future that is sublime."

Whereupon the charming, well-mannered and innocent tyke sums up her attitude toward my attitude with a succinct phrase that I suppose could stand as the epitaph on my long and distinguished career. Like, whenever I explain to Miel that the greatest adventures are in the mind, or that integrity means more than moollah, or that material goods don't matter at all compared to the satisfaction garnered from a paragraph written as if the angels of Shakespeare and the devils of Cormac McCarthy were copulating upon my scribbled page, you know what she replies? "[Bleep] you, John, and the Olympia typewriter you rode in on." [40]

Marriage to a writer, in other words, is not every lover's cup of cliché. "As long as we have each other," the phrase, is not so much a conditional attitude as it is the confident but frustrated stance of writers who govern themselves through innocence and simplicity and wonder and are proudly first to speak out against those pickled in stupidity and lies. But writers are frequently wizards of loneliness—and divorce courts.

Of all persons to quote here, I'll choose a Roman emperor, Marcus Aurelius, often regarded as proto-Christian. "Rather you must, in the train of your thoughts," he writes in *Meditations*,

avoid what is merely casual and without purpose, and above all curiosity and malice; you must habituate yourself only to thoughts about which if someone were suddenly to ask: "What is in your mind now?" you would at once reply, quite frankly, this or that; and so from the answer it would immediately be plain that all was simplicity and kindness . . . [41]

Marcus Aurelius is placing value upon simplicity as a way of dealing with experience and expressing disdain for the deposits of society and history. To me he is more proto-Romantic than proto-Christian, more proto-American than Roman. We, if not he, want the wondering of innocence to be a visionary privilege. A Fellow of King's College Cambridge, the late Tony Tanner, wrote, as follows, in his book *The Reign of Wonder: Naivety and Reality in American Literature*:

> The child's wondering eye offered the romantic writer an avenue back to a reality from which he fast felt himself becoming alienated. By recapturing a naïve vision, he might once again enjoy an untrammeled intimacy with nature. There would be a new reverence, a new quietude, a new sense of total glory.[42]

After surveying American literature from Emerson to Salinger, Tanner concludes:

> What all these writers stress in their various ways is the radical importance of a true way of seeing; the generous, open, even naïve, undulled and reverent eye – as opposed to the self-interested squinting and peering of the greedy utilitarian social eye. Their ideal is an eye of passive wonder.[43]

This very stance of wonder, now that I think about it, appears in my own work. The protagonist of *The Door of the Sad People* has this to say about his vision of life. I confess I agree with it:

> Ever since growing up enough to identify our realm of Sad People – not just the city or region of *los tristes* but the human world of sorrow and folly, of limited knowledge and power—I had conceived of our Door, *la puerta*, both as a boundary and a bondage and as an entrance to a free and higher plane independent of the social order.[44]

The stance of wonder may alienate others from an artist and may motivate them to seek justice by inflicting pain upon him in retaliation for real or merely perceived neglect of personal and social relationships.

The cowboys and cowgirls in wonderland are thinking of the next line or paragraph, not necessarily about love or money.

While I was teaching in London in 1957, I was also trying my hand at painting in oils. Weekends, after packing up a canvas, a box of brushes, turpentine, linseed oil, Windsor & Newton tubes of paint and a small easel, I would take a train to a random destination, paint a cabbage patch for Peter Rabbit fans, put up for the night at an inn, and return to London next day to grade papers. On one of these weekends I took a train from King's Cross to

Cambridge, painted flat-bottomed punts on the Backs of the Cam, and met my future wife.

Jane had during the Second World War been evacuated to Kettlewell in Yorkshire. Her father had been called up and was serving in India. It wasn't an easy time for Jane or her brother and mother, what with shortages of all kinds. They sometimes resorted to eating nettles. After the war her father returned, and the family took up residence in Filey by the North Sea. Exhausted by the war and unhappy, he divorced Jane's mother and shunted Jane off to sidings in private schools for girls, including one school in Switzerland. She was nineteen when he died of a heart attack. When I met her, she had an advanced degree in psychiatric social work, was living in London, and was emerging from group therapy necessitated by memory of all that family trauma. Her mother was living in a thatched-roof cottage near Cambridge, her brother was emigrating to Australia, and the mainstay of emotional support was her father's brother, a thoracic surgeon, Uncle Philip, Nuffield Professor of Surgery at Oxford University.

I and Jane, whom I married in 1957 and divorced in 1974, began with high hopes. We both wanted a family. She gave birth to David and Philip and nourished their growth. Both are alive and well and living in the United States,[45] healthy not least because she insisted on bringing the boys into the world by an intrepid, little-trusted method called "natural childbirth." No drugs, thank you very much.

After I resigned my position at Pennsylvania, Uncle Philip found for us in a village near Oxford a renovated 200-year-old Cotswold-stone farmhouse, two stories, four bedrooms, no dry rot, all mod-con, rent an incredible $25 a week. Nearby Boar's Hill had literary associations: Robert Graves and Lawrence of Arabia had, it was said, once lived there, and "Matthew Arnold's Field" was the inspiration for his poem "The Scholar Gypsy." Six days a week for three years in a study in the farmhouse, I worked on my first novel, quarrying out of a million words a more or less publishable 80,000. The secret to serious writing is a hundred Prufrockian visions and revisions, work so hard you wouldn't wish it on anyone who lacks the fire within. Ann Zwinger, the renowned naturalist, once told an audience of a thousand members of the Western Literature Association that she would rather spend a year scrubbing clean the men's room of the Greyhound bus station in New York City than write a first draft.

A village girl asked little Philip what his father did. Philip, after a pause, said, "He's a doctor of work."

As with any writer, young or old, I needed a first reader. At ocean's length from America I had to be lucky to find a first reader, a mentor, a friend, a facilitator. I got lucky. I met John Wain, in my opinion the leading person of letters of his generation in postwar England.[46] He was urbane, urbanity defined by F.L. Lucas in *Style* as "that form of true politeness which sets men at ease . . . largely based on simple sympathy and unpretentiousness."[47]

He lived with his Welsh wife in a ramshackle house on the Thames River outside Oxford. One evening he telephoned and invited me to join him for an expedition by canoe from his house to the city of Abingdon a dozen or so miles down the river. Next morning, we began paddling. We passed "The Perch," a thatched-roof pub reputed to be the scene of "The Miller's Tale" by Chaucer. Every few miles we stopped at working-class pubs to refresh ourselves with a pint of bitter ale and a game of shove-ha'penny. We paddled, we drank, we stopped and spread ourselves out in the sun on a sandbar. We covered in snatches of conversation literary territory from *Beowulf* to Virginia Woolf. We felt sorry for D.H. Lawrence. Poor David Herbert knew that a certain Anglo-Saxon word beginning with the letter "f" and originally meaning "tenderness" had become so aggressively employed as to be bleeped in polite society, and so in *Lady Chatterley's Lover* he tried to rescue the word for literature. It is still a lost cause. So, John conjectured, when can a conscientious artist employ the f-word? *To sleep with* didn't describe the action, to *have sex* was robotic, to *screw* was mechanical, and to *lay* presented an image of a female upright one moment and hit by a Sherman tank the next. To *make love*? Dubious but keep it around for religious purposes? Quite a tutorial, that.

Unasked, John proposed that we exchange manuscripts. We did that. Several weeks later he telephoned to say we should meet and discuss our works in progress. I motored over to his house. His Welsh wife greeted me warmly and pointed to the garden where John was sitting with my 600-page manuscript in his lap. I already knew that the novel he had given me to read, soon to be published as *A Winter in the Hills*, a love story set in rebellious Wales, was masterful.

Pointing to my manuscript, he said, "I liked it." He went on to say that I had written "ten novels in one." My technique of telling the story of one day through multiple restricted points of view might prove difficult for readers. He was right. I had leaned too much on Virginia Woolf's *Mrs. Dalloway*, James Joyce's *Ulysses*, William Faulkner's *As I Lay Dying* and William Styron's *Lie Down in Darkness*, novels with such techniques. Hoping I hadn't disappointed

John, I thanked him and was leaving when his Welsh wife stopped me at the doorstep and stage-whispered in my ear, "He really liked it!"

Presently I shall be transferring myself from that scene in John Wain's garden to a scene in a former TB sanatorium in Colorado Springs. Writers being so in need of critically sincere friends, mentors, coaches, facilitators, whatever we want to call them, it follows that creativity and literary criticism are two sides of the same coin, each dependent upon the other, each part of a single balancing act. It must also follow that a literary vocation encompasses various activities of a related kind. Pardon the platitude, but *writers must be readers*. In teaching others to write and read, one is also teaching oneself.

Two roads converge.

When inflation crippled England in 1968, I, broke again after having written 600 godawful pages, returned to teaching big-time, as they say, only big-time became full-time/part-time with no more time for writing and still not enough time to earn a living, an insidious trap for an American in what had recently been in England his personal welfare state. Even though the boys were receiving an education almost without equal in the United States, I had to go home to America to pick up a professorship where I had left off. I brought the subject up with Jane, expecting her to accept the necessity of our being together as family. She flew into a fury. "*You* go!" she said, as if husbands and fathers were free to roam as long as they sent support.

"Would you be willing to get a job here and help us out?" I asked, as I recall, gently. She looked at me as if I were out of my mind. I was out of my mind. Why was I staying in a country where people amused themselves by asking me in a sarcastic tone, "How are the colonies today?"

This conversation repeated itself many times over the next few years.

Four nights a week for almost every week in the year I made a forty-mile round-trip to teach a three-hour class in English for the University of Maryland at an American airbase, RAF/USAF Upper Heyford. If I had two classes per each of the many semesters, fifteen or more student airmen per class, I could pay our way. Any fly in that ointment and I was another Wilkins Macawber trying to calculate the importance of sixpence. Since those flies often came buzzing, I tried to get ends to meet by filling up previous "writing" mornings by going to Oxford Polytechnic, lecturing to sweet English girls and boys who were trying to obtain certificates in the publishing industry. From 1968 through 1972, I averaged 90-to-100 preparation and contact hours a week. I was writing nothing and seldom meeting ends.

During that same period the manuscript of my novel was being shopped around in New York by Mac Hyman's former agent, a gentleman of the old school who cared about a writer and his empty purse. After reading my novel, he had met me in London. He believed my prospects were bright. However, for reasons he declared he couldn't fathom, every editor he knew turned us down. Finally, he wrote me a long letter explaining in a kind of agony that he had to let me go. So, it seemed, I was a loser as a writer as well as a breadwinner.

In the Spring of 1972 Jane and I separated on a trial basis. I rented a bed-sitter in Oxford five miles away from the farmhouse. Every weekday morning, I picked the boys up there and drove them to their schools in Abingdon and in late afternoon picked up one or both of them and delivered them home. After that, four evenings a week, I drove twenty-five miles to RAF Upper Heyfod to meet my English classes from seven o'clock to ten o'clock and returned to my digs and played Mozart and Mahler on my record player. I spent another hour preparing for the next morning's class at the Polytechnic. I hit the sack about one. Fridays, I took Jane to buy groceries and to her appointment with a psychiatrist. Saturdays, David had music lessons, Philip played golf, or we went shopping together in town.

I had a supply of unused teabags and, as yet, no eels. I kept my best clothes for classes: flannel trousers, Harris tweed jacket with holes at elbows, preppy-style shirts with button-down collars, silk ties left over from an increasingly remote life in the Ivy League. I was the sartorial equivalent of Custer's Last Stand, fighting a losing battle to avoid becoming a slob.

One afternoon, after dressing up for a night class, subject the *Medea* of Euripides, then picking Philip up and delivering him home, we found Jane out in the courtyard on the inner side of a five-foot-high stone wall. She was watering flowers with a garden hose. As soon as we alighted from the car and entered the courtyard, my beloved Sheltie, "Teapot," rushed barking out of the house and leapt into my arms for a cuddle and lick. Just as I was putting her back down, Jane wheeled about and turned the hose on me full blast, soaking me to the skin beneath my unfashionable gentleman's attire. Because Philip was watching us, I pretended that we grownups were playing a game. I laughed like a clown and danced a sort of Highland fling as I backed out to the courtyard and toward my car. Once out of range of the hose, I waved good-bye to Philip, warned "Teapot" to "stay," wiped cold water from my face, and opened the door of the car.

Then it happened.

Dropping the hose and lifting "Teapot" up, Jane hurled her high over the wall and on to the hard-clay gravel near the car. "Teapot" squealed horribly. Thinking she had broken legs, I ran to her and held her quivering in my arms. After a while, she seemed to be all right. I put her in the car on the passenger seat and got into the car and switched on the ignition and backed the car slowly down the driveway and drove with her beside me to Upper Heyford. All being well, she wouldn't need a vet. She needed me, though, for the rest of her life. I had *Medea* to teach, a play about a mother who murders her children in order to avenge herself on her husband, like me, I suppose, a bum.

The welfare of the boys remained the important question. After a year, I felt confident that they were safe and coping. "Teapot" and I left England and arrived in Colorado Springs on 18 April 1973, to begin a new life, not exactly the one Dante had in mind and yet not one entirely worldly. I was soon to discover that I loved teaching as never before, place, the American West, as never before, and my life in literature as never before. I knew the subject matter as both a specialist and a generalist. I had manuscripts almost ready for publication. Stressed out but not having lost a stance of wonder, I was rediscovering America as New World. I had Rip Van Wrinkle moments. For instance, I had never seen a shopping mall before. Even though I'd lost my Southern accent somewhere in England, I wasn't deracinated. I grew new roots in the West. I was also growing my hair so long that salt-and-pepper ringlets touched my shoulders. Me and the hippies. Sometimes I played my old Martin guitar and sang ballads from both the Southern Appalachians and the Rockies.

Call it the missionary impulse which threads its way through the lives of Blackburns, but I felt at home at the University of Colorado at Colorado Springs (UCCS). Founded in 1965 in buildings of a former TB sanatorium, this little institution for fugitive faculty and some thousand students was perched on bluffs (elevation 6,300 feet) that fronted Pikes Peak (elevation 14,110 feet) from the top of which Katherine Lee Bates had in 1893 composed the opening lines of "America the Beautiful." Although our professors had degrees from Harvard, Yale, Stanford, Berkeley, the Sorbonne and Cambridge, God shed His grace on NORAD, Focus on the Family, and the United States Air Force Academy, not on us. Because our students were "mature"—that is, they came not to party but to learn, and they had daytime jobs, families to support, divorces and the Vietnam War to forget—no one outside our classrooms expected them to amount to anything useful enough to contribute to an alumni fund.

Perfect. Professors met undergraduates in small classes. We conversed on equal terms with one another. There were no vice-chancellors for finance or football. The Humanities, not business and engineering, were still defining the word *education*. Wearing metaphorical robes like Greeks and Romans and sitting under metaphorical olive trees, we learned together in the presence of a mountain and of the Garden of the Gods, both regarded by Native Americans as sacred. At night our bacilli-free buildings, filled with genuine young scholars, were lit up like Depression-era hosiery mills. The library, a box with long horizontal abutments of concrete, bore an unnerving resemblance to bunkers Hitler erected as part of Fortress Europa, and the main building, brilliantly named Main, was still inhabited by bats fluttering behind the peeling plaster walls, still haunted by ghosts of departed lungers, still filled with rattling, whistling noises from steam-heated radiators. The greatest teachers, Socrates and Jesus, would originally, I'm sure, have felt at home at UCCS. Don Quixote would have been enchanted to perceive in our decrepit wind-mills an Alhambra and in a pregnant hippie from communes in the mountains the incomparable Dulcinea del Toboso. That was the way it was. Nowadays UCCS is aiming for 20,000 students and emphasis on business and technology.

The West, I discovered, was rich in writers, poor in publishers, so I founded an annual literary magazine. Almost at once, quality poems and stories began to fill my *Writers' Forum* mail-box.

My creative writing class was meeting on the top floor of Main one afternoon in October 1973. A student with hair down to his hairless chest and a pouch of pot around his neck was seated by a window and pointing. "Hey, Dr. Blackburn," he said, "there's this black dude down yonder back from 'Nam who writes po'try." The word *poetry* arranged my missionary impulse into a charge. "Break," I said. I rushed down four flights of stairs, emerged into sunlight, and approached a small group of students who were gathered around the probable black poet who was smiling gently and pushing spectacles off the bridge of his nose. I introduced myself ("Alex") and explained my rude intrusion ("I have a class in writing"). We shook hands.

"Yusef," he said. His voice, rich and deep and slow, resonated with tones from the South.

"You write poetry, I'm told."

Yusef grinned boyishly, "Gosh," he said, adjusting spectacles.

"I mean," I pressed, "I'd be more than happy to read it. With your permission."

He told me he would deliver his poems to my office. As I turned to go, I thought to ask, "You're not by any chance an English major?"

"Distributed Studies," he replied with an enigmatic smile and a tone of embarrassment. "Psychology. It's a trip."

Next day he dropped a thick sheaf of poems off at my office. There were dozens of them. If Yusef was as talented as he seemed to be, what on earth was he doing on the poor man's Magic Mountain? When I read the poems that evening, I couldn't answer that question. One thing, however, was beyond any doubt: he was a true poet.

His name was Yusef Komunyakaa.

I knew I would be telling the story for years to come, how an accidental teacher can offer encouragement, how *Writers' Forum* enabled me to publish Yusef's poems in the first three volumes, how those poems attracted praise from National-Book-Award-winning novelist John Williams, future Faulkner-Award-winning novelist John Edgar Wideman, and how Yusef earned a teaching assistantship to study at Colorado State University under poet Bill Tremblay. Yusef Komunyakaa would go on to win the Pulitzer Prize for Poetry. In *Neon Vernacular* were revised versions of some poems he had shown me in 1973.

A few years ago, while Inés and I were in New York, Yusef came up from Princeton where he was at that time a professor of English. We stopped for coffee at a restaurant near Columbia University. With very good grace and an air of diffidence Yusef mentioned to Inés, with a sideways glance at me, that his new book, *Blue Notes*, had been dedicated to me.

"That's very handsome of you," I managed to blurt out, never having dreamed of such an honor.

"You saved me," he said, a blank expression on his face. There was, I hoped, humor in the proceedings.

"Tell us," Inés said.

Yusef leaned conspiratorially over his coffee cup and said, "I was going to become a psychologist."[48]

How easy it is for parents and teachers, among others, to forget the meaning to students of encouragement, the unconscious flow of caring!

In 1975 what I didn't know about Inés and didn't need to know bowed down to what I beheld in the light of my joy. I didn't know her name. I didn't know that Dr. Inés Dölz Henry was from Santiago de Chile, that she had come to the United States in 1962 at the invitation of St. Mary's College, University of Notre Dame, in order to teach Spanish and Latin American language and literature, that she held a doctorate degree in those subjects, that she was a poet and author, that she had a little girl from a first marriage, and that she had passed up a permanent position on the faculty of a top prep school in order to become a professor at UCCS.

It was the middle of August. I had just returned from my annual summer visit with David and Philip in England and was heartened by their progress and well-being. I had taken them to the Isle of Iona where Western civilization had begun to emerge from the Dark Ages, a theme I could relate to.[49] My salary of $12,500 was by now enough to enable me to send them and their mother $8,000. The first novel was revised and finally finished. My readings in Joseph Campbell's books on mythology were enabling me to focus new attention on the origins of the modern novel in Spain. I could rationalize my late development as a writer. Cervantes (1547-1616) had completed *Don Quixote* in 1605. Alain René Lesage (1668-1747) had worked on *Gil Blas* from the age of forty-seven to the age of sixty-seven. Daniel Defoe (1660? -1731) hadn't published *Moll Flanders* until 1722. Voltaire (1694-1778) had been almost seventy when he began *Candide*. Wasn't there a lot to be said for cutting wisdom teeth?

There was. But there was also a lot to be said about becoming a mute inglorious Milton in a potter's field.

The faculty of the College of Letters, Arts & Sciences had been invited to gather on the lawn of a convent in the foothills of Pikes Peak in order to discuss "Teaching and Learning."

"You can't go," I explained to "Teapot" in our cottage on a slope in Manitou Springs. "I've been talking to you for three years, teaching you to stop pooping on the rug, and you haven't learned a thing."

I drove my '64 Dodge over to Saint Somebody's, parked, and spotted a group of people squatting in the shade of a distant wall and giving attention to a speaker who must have been a professor because she wore torn jeans and sprouted a head of hair like a mushroom cloud. Perhaps because the professors, unlike "Teapot," seemed to be housebroken, I went and squatted down in the front row of the group just as the speaker was asking for questions.

Then it happened.

From behind me came a voice soft as music, a Spanish voice. Spanish, as I knew from a folksong, is the loving tongue.

I turned my head.

There she was.

How pure you are by sunlight or a fallen night.[50]

III

CHAPTER 4

Mythology and the Modern Novel

While I was growing up, the Western European thought that character-izes and informs literature of the twelfth century was not as far from my mind as youth spent on Tobacco Road might lead one to believe. A walk of twenty minutes from home led me to the West Campus of Duke Univer-sity, its "collegiate Gothic" architecture making an impression on me beyond the merely exorbitant in a landscape of red clay and loblolly pines. Moreover, my father had published in 1939 *The Architecture of Duke University*, and my mother possessed *Mont-Saint-Michel and Chartres* by Henry Adams, both of which books I read by the age of twelve.[51] The style of stained-glass windows of Duke Chapel had been influenced, I knew, by those in the Gothic cathe-dral in Chartres. As for literature, although I was immersed in the stories of King Arthur and didn't know the difference between the fifth and the twelfth centuries, I sensed that there was something curiously antiauthoritarian about the relationship of Guinevere and Sir Lancelot, romance, I learned years later, imported into the Christian twelfth-century's literature from Celtic sources.

By the age of seventeen I knew just barely enough about European history to feel the omnipresence of oppression in the twelfth century. The Crusades had apparently been fueled superficially by faith, mostly by a lust for plunder. The Inquisition under Pope Innocent III had exterminated a million Albigenses in southern France.

I had studied Latin at Andover and had been coerced by necessity—a college entrance requirement—to read Virgil's *Aeneid* in the original. Even though the subjunctive mood had me flummoxed, I loved the poem and would later draw upon its theme of imperialism in a novel about the Atomic Age, *The Voice of the Children in the Apple Tree*. Beyond that, I was exposed to a few works in English and American literature, almost all of them, *The Scarlet Letter* for example, smelling of nineteenth-century lamps. I was not to read Chaucer and Shakespeare until I went to college. Chaucer appeared in the fourteenth century, Shakespeare in the late sixteenth. The closest I got to twelfth-century poets and then to early fourteenth-century Dante was in footnotes to T.S. Eliot's *The Waste Land*. Had I, perhaps, been introduced to *The Cantos* of Ezra Pound—I wasn't—I might have been prepared to listen carefully and humbly to Provençal literature, especially troubadour biographies.[52] In 1959 at the University of Virginia professors led us to believe that literature of the Middle Ages was largely irrelevant to "real" scholarship, a narrow field beginning with Chaucer, Shakespeare, Spenser, and Milton. The professor who specialized in the history of the English novel mentioned mid-sixteenth-century *Lazarillo de Tormes* as if it were an invertebrate mollusk. A Virginian with a flushed countenance and deep throat, he pronounced *Quixote* as "quicksut."

Not until 1968 in England would I recognize in the twelfth century the genesis of a world culture—*our* World Culture.

A part-time adjunct professor for the University of Maryland's European Division, I was handed the syllabus for a course called "Great Books" and told to teach it in a semester of eight weeks to noncommissioned officers in the United States Air Force who were often on 48-hour NATO alerts and believed that the way to solve problems with Commies was to "nuke 'em." Books written in English were happily excluded; the Great Books were translations of Classical and continental works ranging from ca. 800 B.C. to the late nineteenth century. My life as an amateur polymath began. Although I taught *The Book of Job* in the King James Version, a tragedy with a weird happy ending, I had to refrain from revealing that it is possibly a Buddhist text! The author of *The Odyssey* probably never existed as the blind beggar of tradition. One scholar thought it was originally sung by an eighteen-year-old girl on an island off the coast of Albania! Why would my airmen dig *Agamemnon*? I figured they would. It's about a stupid general whose wife is cheating on him while he's in Troy nuking Asians. What about *Oedipus Rex*? My airmen, whose language was often filled with expressions about "mother," would get the incest idea.

Only, there was the problem of the text of *The Romance of Tristan and Iseult*, dated in 1945, first published in 1913, the text said to be "retold by Joseph Bédier, translated by Hilaire Belloc, and completed by Paul Rosenfelt."[53] Belloc, a French-born English writer who died in 1953, was translating from stories retold by Bédier, and Bédier was bothered by or surreptitiously turned on by depictions of sexual intercourse in literature. There are five literary versions based on distillations from pagan Celtic myth. The earliest version of the Tristan story dates to about 1150 A.D. It was followed by the versions of Thomas of Britain (composed 1165-1170), Eilhart von Oberge (composed 1180-1190), the Norman Frenchman Béroul (composed 1191-1205) and Gottfried von Strassburg (composed 1210). Gottfried was, I found, a great poet, a worthy precursor of Dante. If Bédier had followed Gottfried he might have comprehended compassionate love and honor, but his orthodoxy, in my opinion, blinded him to what Gottfried made obvious: Tristan and Iseult follow the dictates of the heart.

I'll give two examples. When King Mark demands that Iseult of Ireland marry him, he specifies that her maid, who accompanies her and his loyal vassal Tristan on the sea voyage to England, bring along a love potion, in other words, an aphrodisiac suitable for dysfunctional monarchs. King Mark wants to swallow this Viagra of the Dark Ages on the wedding night. Tristan and Iseult accidentally drink the potion and surrender to desire. When we read the Bédier compilation, he wants us to believe that the drug is responsible for passion, and that, therefore, the lovers' concupiscence is adulterous because Iseult is betrothed—already bound by a sacramental duty. If you believe this interpretation, you have a friend in St. Augustine. A Manichaean during the most formative years of his life, he bequeathed to Christians since the fifth century the bleak notion that life is evil and sex is sin. If on the other hand you believe in dictates of the heart, you have a friend in Gottfried who regards the drug as a symbol for a full, compassionate love being first awakened. Here's the second example. Iseult, now Queen, is out in the woods in a grotto, sleeping alongside Tristan on what is called a "crystalline bed." Back in his smelly castle, Mark stops scratching his millimetric brow long enough for the worm of suspicion to persuade him he's a cuckold. He dashes off into the wilderness, sneaks up on the lovers, and sees that Tristan's razor-sharp sword has been placed on the bed so as physically to separate them. Presumably wincing at the thought of a naked couple's rolling over on the sword, Mark votes for acquittal. Bédier, however, is not going to let Tristan and Iseult get away with what seems the subterfuge of adulterers. Had he bothered to accept Gottfried's version of the incident, he would have realized that the lovers are, in truth, symbolically "married" and graced by a nobility in their love long after the effects of the potion have worn off. The crystalline bed is a symbol of purity.

A great deal of rubbish has been piled on *Tristan and Iseult* by scholars still mired in the moral order which condemned them in the first place. In *Passion and Society*, for instance, Denis de Rougemont traces to the Tristan story 800 years of popular extramarital affairs.[54] Sanctified by the Church, marriage is regarded as a sacrament, but in the Middle Ages it was in fact little more than a secular obscenity involving property rights. While there is no doubt that adultery is and long has been a theme in literature and movies, the Tristan story—once we follow Gottfried and understand how the conventional language of "marriage" and "adultery" is being subverted—is not responsible for the history of illicit affairs. To the contrary, once the prickly shrubbery of irony has been penetrated, we see that Tristan and Iseult are in authentic terms married indeed, the specious ceremony with King Mark notwithstanding. Gottfried apparently didn't trust indoctrinated readers to understand this "heresy," so he addressed his version of the story to "noble hearts." Probably we today should substitute for the word "noble," associated with birth and rank, some words we live and die for in the modern age, words such as "individual," "free," and "true" now modifying "hearts." The story of Tristan and Iseult is a story of genuine love and compassion.

In Oxford in 1968 when I was struggling with the problem of interpreting *The Romance of Tristan and Iseult* for my students, I happened to stop by Blackwell's bookstore for the sheer pleasure of browsing through shelves of books I couldn't afford to buy. About to leave the store, I glanced at a case-bound book with an intriguing title, *Creative Mythology*. On impulse I plucked it off the shelf. Noting its price, six pounds ten shillings, I almost returned it to the shelf but didn't. Because I wasn't buying, I took my time flipping through hundreds of pages expecting to find no swans among geese. And was hooked. The foundation for World Culture lies, so to say, in the story of Tristan and Iseult and in the real-life story of Abélard and Héloise, this master of mythology, Joseph Campbell, was telling me. Could it be that the Monumental Sky-God Culture of 7,000 years' duration began to change in the twelfth century of all godawful centuries? I bought the book.

Throughout his career Campbell was concerned with historical transformations of those imagined forms through which men everywhere have sought to relate themselves to the wonder of existence. Whereas a profound respect for inherited forms has generally suppressed innovation, in our recent West since the middle of the twelfth century an accelerating disintegration has been undoing the formidable orthodox tradition in that century and releasing the creative power of individuals, especially in the fields of literature, secular philosophy, and the arts. A new kind of revelation has become the actual spiritual guide and structuring force of civilization. Now it's the individual who has an experience of his own, and if his realization has been of a certain depth and import, his communication will have, Campbell asserts, the value and force of living myth. In Christian Europe, already in the twelfth century, beliefs no longer universally held were universally enforced, resulting in a dissociation of professed from actual experience.

Campbell adheres to Gottfried's version of the Tristan story. He explains that Gottfried's crucial concept opens inward toward the mystery of character, destiny, and worth, and at the same time outward, toward the world and the wonder of beauty, where it sets the lovers at odds, however, with the moral order. The principle of individuality is thereby engaged due to radical dissociation and collision of individual and group values. In other words, the power of love in its most poignant form elevates us to a spirituality opposed to orthodoxy. Love asserts a oneness surpassing in terms of consciousness the controls of archaic mythologies, the ones that thrust the spirit upwards to a "space" in faith-based cosmography, as ziggurats, pyramids, cathedrals and the structure of Dante's *Divine Comedy* do. In Monumental Culture the implied locus of divinity had been for thousands of years aloft, with the heavens as center of awe and wonder, whereas in the new World Culture the center is the human heart.

This brief summary of Campbell's *Creative Mythology* serves as an introduction to modern literature, to the modern novel in particular, but I'll reserve further exposition of mythology and the modern novel until after I've introduced Abélard's *Historia calamitatum* and Héloise's letters as given us with commentary by Campbell.

The story of Tristan and Iseult was enacted in reality in the lives of Abélard (1079-1142) and Héloise (1101?-1164?). At the very moment, so to say, when Héloise transfers her love of God to her love of a man, "a new kind of revelation," as Campbell says, "has become the actual spiritual guide and structuring force of the civilization." It was no casual moment. A person of her times, she had to believe that everlasting torments of Hell awaited her, and there was already a living torment, Abélard's coldness to her after their separation. If I were to imagine the face of Héloise, there would be at first glance the face of the Virgin in Michelangelo's *Pietà*, sad, serene, loving and longing, and then at second glance a face of anguish and defiance and yet also self-abnegation prostrate before a lover.

I trust the following extensive extracts from Campbell's *Creative Mythology* will not only confirm my indebtedness to him but also inspire writers and readers to see themselves as part of a vast empowerment of humanity.

> Marriage in the Middle Ages was an affair largely of convenience. Moreover, girls betrothed in childhood for social, economic, or political ends, were married very young, and often to much older men, who invariably took their property rights in the women they had married very seriously. They might be away for years on Crusade; the wife was to remain inviolate, and if for any reason the worm Suspicion happened to have entered to gnaw the husband's brain, his blacksmith might be summoned up to fit an iron girdle of chastity to the mortified young wife's pelvic basin. The Church sanctified these sordid property rights, furthermore, with all the weight of Hell, Heaven, eternity, and the coming of Christ in glory on the day of judgment ... So that, against all of this, the wakening of a woman's heart to love was in the Middle Ages a grave and really terrible disaster, not only for herself, for whom torture, and fire were in prospect, but also for her lover; and not only here on earth but also—and more horribly—in the world to come, forever. Abélard was thirty-eight, Héloise eighteen, and the year 1118 A.D. "There was in Paris a young girl named "Héloise, the niece of a canon Fulbert," we read in the rueful autobiographical letter known as Abélard's *Historia calamitatum* . . .

> Now it may or may not be relevant that Abélard, like Tristan of the legend, was born in Celtic Brittany, where, in those years, that oft-told tale of illicit love was in the making which (in Gottfried's phrase) was "bread to all noble hearts." Abélard, like Tristan, was a harpist of renown: his songs composed to Héloise were sung throughout the young Latin Quarter. And, like Tristan, he was given the task of tutoring the young lady, who, like the maid Isolt, was comparable (in other words, again, of Gottfried) "only to the Sirens with their lodestone, who draw to themselves stray ships."

> > To the agitation of many a heart [wrote Gottfried of the maid Isolt] she sang at once openly and secretly, by the

ways of both ear and eye. The melody sung openly, both
abroad and with her tutor, was of her own sweet voice and
the strings' soft sound that openly and clearly rode through
the kingdom of the ears, down deep, into the heart. But the
secret song was her marvelous beauty itself, which covertly
and silently slipped through the windows of the eyes, and
in many noble hearts spread a magic that immediately
made thoughts captive and fettered them with yearning and
yearning's stress.

Love was in the air in that century of the troubadours, shaping loves
no less than tales; but the lives, specifically and only, of those of noble
heart, whose courage in their knowledge of love announced the great
theme that was in time to become the characteristic signal of our
culture: the courage, namely, to affirm against tradition whatever
knowledge stands confirmed in one's own controlled experience. For
the first of such creative knowledges in the destiny of the West was
of the majesty of love, against the supernatural utilitarianism of the
sacramental system of the Church. And the second was of reason. So
it can be truly said that the first published manifesto of this new age
of the world, the age of the self-reliant individual, appeared at the
first dawn of the most creative century of the Gothic Middle Ages,
in the love and the noble love letters of the lady Héloise to Abélard.
For when she discovered herself pregnant, her lover, in fear, spirited
her off to his sister's place in Brittany; and when she had there given
birth to his son—whom they christened Astralabius—Abélard, as
the calamitous letter tells, proposed to her that they should marry.
However, as we read, returning to Abélard's words:

> She strongly disapproved and urged two reasons against the
> marriage, to wit, the danger and the disgrace in which it
> would involve me.

> She swore—and so it proved—that no satisfaction would
> ever appease her uncle. She asked how she was to have
> any glory through me when she should have made me
> inglorious and should have humiliated both herself and
> me. What penalties would the world extract from her if she
> deprived it of such a luminary; what curses, what damage
> to the Church, what lamentations of philosophers, would
> follow on this marriage! How indecent, how lamentable
> would it be for a man whom nature had made for all,

to declare that he belonged to one woman, and subject himself to such shame!

The letter, continuing, next recounts some of the arguments urged by Héloise in dissuasion.

From her soul [wrote Abélard to his reader], she detested this marriage, which would be so utterly ignominious for me, and a burden to me. She expatiated on the disgrace and inconvenience of matrimony for me and quoted the Apostle Paul exhorting men to shun it. If I would not take the apostle's advice or listen to what the saints had said regarding the matrimonial yoke, I should at least pay attention to the philosophers—to Theophrastus's words upon the intolerable evils of marriage, and to the refusal of Cicero to take a wife after he had divorced Terentia, when he said that he could not devote himself to a wife and philosophy at the same time. "Or," she continued, "laying aside the disaccord between study and a wife, consider what a married man's establishment would be to you. What sweet accord there would be between the schools and domestics, between copyists and cradles, between books and distaffs, between pen and spindle! Who, engaged in religious or philosophical meditations, could endure a baby's crying and the nurse's ditties stilling it, and all the noise of servants? Could you put up with the dirty ways of children? The rich can, you say, with their palaces and apartments of all kinds; their wealth does not feel the expense or the daily care and annoyance. But I say, the state of the rich is not that of philosophers; nor have men entangled in riches and affairs any time for the study of Scripture or philosophy. The renowned philosophers of old, despising the world, fleeing rather than relinquishing it, forbade themselves all pleasures, and reposed in the embraces of philosophy ... If laymen and Gentiles, bound by no profession of religion, lived thus, surely you, a clerk and a canon, should not prefer low pleasures to sacred duties, nor let yourself be sucked down by this Charybdis and smothered in filth inextricably. If you do not value the privilege of a clerk, at least defend the dignity of a philosopher. If reverence for God be despised, still let love of decency temper immodesty . . ."

Finally [Abélard continued to his friend] she said that it would be dangerous for me to take her back to Paris; it was more becoming to me, and sweeter to her, to be called my mistress, so that affection alone might keep me hers and not the binding power of any matrimonial chain; and if we should be separated for a time, our joys at meeting would be the dearer for their rarity. When at last with all her persuasions and dissuasions she could not turn me from my folly, and could not bear to offend me, with a burst of tears she ended in these words: "One thing is left: in the ruin of us both the grief which follows shall not be less than the love which went before."

"Nor did she here lack the spirit of prophecy," the poor man added in comment; for the world knows what then occurred. Leaving their son in Brittany in the care of Abélard's sister, the couple returned to Paris and were married in the presence of the canon Fulbert, her uncle, who, however, still resenting the seduction, deflowering, and marriage of his niece, retaliated like a savage. "Having bribed my servant," Abélard wrote, "they came upon me by night, when I was sleeping, and took on me a vengeance as cruel and irretrievable as it was vile and shameful!" The canon Fulbert and his footpads had turned Abélard into an eunuch—who, however, in the spirit of a true and penitent Christian, finally was able to reflect in his confessional letter, years later: "I thought of my ruined hopes and glory, and then saw that by God's just judgment I was punished where I had most sinned, and that Fulbert had justly avenged treachery with treachery." That is the first part of this cruel story. The second carries us further; for Abélard, in his shame, entered the monastery of Saint Denis as a monk, and Héloise, in obedience to his wish, the convent of Argenteuil as a nun. Ten years of silence followed, whereafter, from the convent to the monastery came a letter with the following superscription:

To her master, rather to a father, to her husband, rather to a brother, his maid or rather a daughter, his wife or rather sister, to Abélard, Héloise . . .

And therein the following, among much more of the kind, was to be read:

Thou knowest, dearest—and who knows not?—how much I lost in thee, and that an infamous act of treachery robbed me of thee and of myself at once ...Love turned to madness and cut itself off from hope of that which alone it sought, when I obediently changed my garb and my heart too in order that I might prove thee sole owner of my body as well as of my spirit. God knows, I have ever sought in thee only thyself, desiring simply thee and not what was thine. I asked no matrimonial contract, I looked for no dowry; not my pleasure, not my will, but thine have I striven to fulfill. And if the name of wife seemed holier or more potent, the word mistress [*amica*] was always sweeter to me, or even— be not angry! —concubine or harlot; for the more I lowered myself before thee, the more I hoped to gain thy favor, and the less I should hurt the glory of thy renown.

I call God to witness that if Augustus, the master of the world, would honor me with marriage and invest me with equal rule, it would still seem to me dearer and more honorable to be called thy strumpet than his empress. He who is rich and powerful is not the better: that is a matter of fortune, this of merit. And she is venal who marries a rich man sooner than a poor man, and yearns for a husband's riches rather than himself. Such a woman deserves pay and not affection. She is not seeking the man but his goods, and would wish, if possible, to prostitute herself to one still richer . . .

The nun, now the abbess of her convent, reviews the young love sense of the tender lamb and middle-aged, ravenous wolf: "What queen did not envy me my joys and couch?" she wrote to her shattered lover of yore.

There were in you two qualities by which you could draw the soul of any woman, the gift of poetry and the gift of singing, gifts which other philosophers had lacked. As a distraction from labor, you composed love-songs both in meter and in rhyme, which for their sweet sentiment and music have been sung and resung and have kept your name in every mouth. Your sweet melodies do not permit even the illiterate to forget you. Because of these gifts, women sighed for your love. And, as these songs sang of our loves, they quickly spread my name in many lands, and made me the envy of my sex. What excellence of mind or body did not adorn your youth?

That had been the lover then; whereas now, as she reminds him, during the ten years of their separation she has not received from that lover a single written line. "Tell me," she wrote, "one thing," and here she drove her dart:

> Why, after our conversion, commanded by thyself, did I drop into oblivion, to be no more refreshed by speech of thine or letter? Tell me, I say, if you can, or I will say what I feel and what everyone suspects: desire rather than friendship drew you to me, lust rather than love. So, when desire ceased, whatever you were manifesting for its sake likewise vanished. This, beloved, is not so much my opinion as the opinion of all. Would it were only mine and that thy love might find defenders to argue away my pain. Would that I could invent some reason to excuse you and also cover my cheapness. Listen, I beg, to what I ask, and it will seem small and very easy to you. Since I am cheated of your presence, at least put vows in words, of which you have a store, and so keep before me the sweetness of thine image . . . When little more than a girl I took the hard vows of a nun, not from piety but at your command. If I merit nothing from thee, how vain I deem my labor! I can expect no reward from God, as I have done nothing from love of Him . . . God knows, at your command I would have followed or preceded you to fiery places. For my heart is not with me, but with thee.

Obviously, the man had [profaned a shrine] and the same man, now a eunuch monk, was about to do so again. For the shrine of the abbess Héloise was to a deity unrecognized by the offices of Abélard's theology: an actual experience, namely, of love, not for an abstraction but for a person; a flame of love in which lust and religion are equally consumed, so that, in fact, Abélard was her god. In her own words . . . not the natural, animal urgencies of lust, not the supernatural, angelic desire to glow forever in the beatific vision, but the womanly, purely human experience of love for a specific living being, and the courage to burn for that love were to be the kingdom and the glory of a properly human life.[55]

The mythogenetic zone having moved from the heavens to the heart, with Experience juxtaposed to Authority, the stage was set for the eventual appearance of the modern novel. I doubt there were "modern" novels, as we know them through their craft of temporal disposition, composed between 1118 A.D. and 1554 A.D. when *Lazarillo de Tormes* appeared. We know of wonderful fictions by Boccaccio (1313-1375) and by Erasmus (1466? -1536), but, as far as I have been able to tell, a novelistic form consisting of elements of emerging World Culture simply doesn't arrive until 1554, probably for good reason. Is it not a sad but revealing omission that the author of *Lazarillo* remains anonymous to this day? Savonarola was excommunicated and burned as a heretic. Galileo, who lived well into the seventeenth century, recanted under pressure from the Church. In Spain any Jew who was not a *converso*, someone forcibly converted to Christianity, had to fear for his life. The theory that the author of *Lazarillo* was a *converso* is certainly worth considering, for, as Campbell makes clear in general terms, a dissociation of professed from actual experience was increasingly being felt by individuals. *Lazarillo* expresses exactly such a feeling, the feeling of a lost soul.[56]

At first glance *Lazarillo* seems an imitation of Lucius Apuleius's *Metamorphoses*, usually known to us in the English-speaking world as *The Golden Ass*. Written about 150 A.D. and translated into Spanish about 1510, this somewhat "novelistic" Latin narrative employs the technique of autobiographical point of view. So does *Lazarillo*. The character of Lucius, however, is no Lazarus, who looks back at his "little Lazarus" boyhood self from the perspective of a fully conscious individual. Lucius has no "character" in our sense of the word. Literally transformed into an ass, he is not even human nor has time effected his metamorphosis.

"What we call the self, the person, or individual," Hans Meyerhoff declares in *Time in Literature*, "is experienced and known only against the background of the succession of temporal moments and changes constituting his biography."[57] An individual, Lazarus is conscious of a moral order which *deformed* him in his formative years. No rebel against corrupt society, he mirrors it. He boasts about his hollow "success" in creating an identity out of appearances. The "I" of his autobiography is isolated and loveless. It will take the omniscient point of view in *Don Quixote* fifty years later to give us the "we" embedded in novels for centuries to come, but the loneliness of the long-distance antihero will partially reappear in novels such as Herman Melville's *The Confidence-Man*, Mark Twain's *Huckleberry Finn*, and Ralph Ellison's *Invisible Man* as the gap again is felt to widen between self and society.

The psychologist Julian Jaynes describes our own age as one in which people merely pay lip service to deities not truly known inwardly for a very long time:

> We have our houses and gods which record our births, define us, marry us, and bury us, receive our confessions and intercede with the gods to forgive us our trespasses. Our laws are based upon values which without their divine pendency would be empty and unenforceable. Our national mottoes and hymns of state are usually divine invocations. Our kings, presidents, judges, and officers begin their tenure with oaths to the now silent deities taken upon the writings of those who have last heard them.[58]

Jaynes finds hope in the full human consciousness that has arrived, at least in westernized cultures, to fill the void left in our minds by the departure of noisy, now silent, deities. His hypothesis with important implications for literature is this: in ancient times the mind was divided into two "rooms," one room for humans, one room for gods. In stories which have come down to us from Homer and the Old Testament he extracts evidence to support his claims about a "bicameral" mind. In *The Iliad* and in *The Odyssey*, a god or goddess appears to a hero as if out of a mist and intercedes in actions with demands he is obliged to obey. According to Jaynes, once the god's room is emptied, humans thereafter become responsible for causality, and anyone today who believes he is conversing with "god" may be viewed as a hallucinating schizophrenic. Since the deity isn't "there" any longer but may still ride the brain, the person so obsessed or possessed is lugging the mythology of Monumental Culture back into World Culture. His authority, assuming a posture of belief in ancient texts, is in all probability vested in archaic morality, coercive government, and anthropomorphic deities.

Experience is up against Authority. The literary form especially adapted to confront de-humanizing threats, externalized and internalized, is the modern novel, the quintessential technique of which is conflict—a war in which humanity itself is at stake.

CHAPTER 5

Experience, Imagination, and Revolt

Write about experience. Write about what you know. How often we are told this, first perhaps by a teacher, later by our own inner voice. The advice is by no means clear. Are we, like Hemingway, to celebrate a cowboy-code, to chase after wars and wild game, and to pay homage to bullfighters before we have the experience to write about them? If so, how are we going to explain Emily Dickinson, who wrote thousands of poised and intricate poems without venturing far from her father's house in Amherst? True, we must sometimes get away from our Amherst in order to focus feelings and refresh the sense of wonder. We might, like Thomas Wolfe, conclude that we can't go home again. On the other hand, we might, like Faulkner, conclude that the little postage stamp of earth called "home" provides enough experience to inspire a lifetime of writing. Either way, experience is something we already possess, though it may be hidden from consciousness, like the roots of sleep.

Beginning writers, in particular, are wary of probing and quarrying-out the deep and possibly painful experiences that might threaten an already tentative self-identity with such mysteries as sex and death unless emotion is contained in art and is no longer identifiable as the writer's self or surrogate self—a critical problem, by the way, with Wolfe's rhapsodic, semi-autobiographical *Look Homeward, Angel*. Lacking confidence in art, beginning writers are prone to turn away from self-discovery and indulge in something vaguely called "self-expression," a kind of detour around emotion and in the direction of intergalactic space, of frontier towns where everyone is quick

on the draw, or of the family life of Minnie Mouse. Of course, we all share
a compulsion to get away from reality and to soar on wings of fantasy to a
world elsewhere. As I shall explain later, the American imagination thrives on
creation of new worlds. But there comes a time when your spaceship develops
an oil leak, when your cowboy has such a bad case of flatulence that even the
vilest galoot in Yellow Sky won't get close enough to fight him, and when
Minnie Mouse gets coked to the whiskers on dope. Continued avoidance of
real experience means you are apt to fly, not to outer space, but to pieces.

Wallace Stegner has written that writers born in the American West
face a special problem. They are "born square . . . a sort of majority product, a
belated and provincial one at that, formed by majority attitudes and faiths."[59]
Although western-born writers are healthy animals in what until very recently was an essentially pre-industrial, pre-urban society, they are none the less
lured from the land they know and persuaded that literature is concerned with
what they don't know, the lives of exiles, junkies, and hustlers, of victims of
holocausts, of poverty and the class struggle. Poor westerner, he finds dignity
and hope in living. Still, it seems, he must learn to suffer quiet desperation in
order to be "literary," perhaps imitate Mary McCarthy and write scathingly
sophisticated accounts of the rot in Denmark. She was born in Seattle.

But the real problem is not the lack or inadequacy of experience; it
is, rather, the delayed arrival of revelation. Like Molière's bourgeois gentleman who was astonished to discover he'd been speaking prose all his life, a
writer has to open his eyes to the immediate and obvious. There is a scene in
Faulkner's *Absalom, Absalom!* when young Thomas Sutpen has been rebuffed
at a plantation owner's door and flees to a cave where he reviews the whole of
his life. It was "like when you pass through a room fast and look at all of the
objects in it and you turn and go back through the room again and look at
all the objects from the other side and you find out you had never seen them
before."[60] Humanity needs to be seen "from the other side." Recall Joseph
Conrad's *Heart of Darkness*. After finding Kurtz in Africa, Marlowe realizes
that this European who has reverted to savagery is still, at the last gasp, human—unspeakably free but capable of understanding his own damnation,
hence a creature worthy of compassion. Marlowe's quest for self-knowledge
is a journey beyond the environments of Western civilization and into the
"heart" of humanity's capacities for good and evil. A writer's quest is a similar awakening to the glory and horror of being, a recognition of one's self in

the human image in both a specific and a universal sense. Whereas specific experiences are infinitely varied, universal experiences are those that bleed to a prick and occur in a visible world. Compassion, pity, humility, fortitude, grief, endurance: these are some of them, and you will find them anywhere, even in sunny California.

Because serious writing beyond entertainment and escape is self-discovery, not self-expression, we need to surpass our "real" experience. This is the point where imagination comes into play: imagination can approach a particular object to reveal it in its fullness, the net of analogies in which each object reaches out to another object.

Some experiences are more bound up than others with the feelings and meanings that enshrine the spirit. These are the experiences of the heart's blood, the ones that have absorbed our attention, often from an early age, the ones that have bestowed on us our awareness, the ones inside of which we have grown. They are spiritual shrines where the literary gods abide, those images so imbued with strong emotions as to have the power to crack us open and to fuel the long endeavor of art. Probably in your childhood years you stood still and looked about in awe and terror at the mystery of being until you had your fill of time and place. Then when you went through the rite of passage into youth and were figuratively reborn into the life of struggle and fulfillment, the world, in Wordsworth's phrase, was "too much with us." You looked back upon childhood as if from afar, as if, again in Wordsworth's phrase, "there hath past away a glory from the earth." Still there in your mind's eye, however, are the enshrined images awaiting your acknowledgement. As James Joyce discovered in exile when he was writing *Dubliners*, Dublin had never been lost. You had little idea before just how mysterious is the mystery of yourself, and now you must be prepared, like Faulkner's Sutpen, "to go back through the room again and look at all the objects from the other side." It is going to be difficult, but you have to be faithful to the wounds of life and not be discouraged from your task by a sense of your nakedness before social, economic, and religious authorities of the tribe. You are breaking away from the tribe's daylight world, submerging in the sea of images, beginning your pilgrimage to the shrines where the truth of your experience lies. Out of this submergence, this pilgrimage, you may surface with poems and stories. Oddly, you will be told by the tribe—you may even tell yourself—that you're wasting your time away from the "real" world, that "truth" is just "information," something to be retrieved from a database and put to use. But it is the tribe that lives blindly in the world created out of myths, lost on the surface of reality, emotions suppressed, with reason itself unable to recognize the impracticality—indeed the insanity—of the pursuit of wealth and power.

The feelings of time and place that spirit enshrines return to us in memory and dream, the images transformed in pattern and significance and pliant enough to be molded to new, unifying shape. The power of the image lies in its capacity to beget other images, to expand from the Big Bang of deep feeling to the creation of unsuspected stars. The containment of this power is art. What begins as a strong emotion-charged image-particle is gradually externalized into form, so that the poem or the story finally assumes a life of its own, irrespective of autobiographical origins. How do you know when the poem or story is finished? When you're able to see it from all sides. When it is no longer "you." When your "you" is, as John Donne said centuries ago, "involved with mankind," the one "for whom the bell tolls." When mortal time is no longer quite the old winged chariot hurrying near, but an element arrested in the mystery of here-and-now. That's when.

One of the greatest of American novels, Faulkner's *The Sound and the Fury* originated in an image of a little girl who is climbing a tree and whose brothers observe her muddy underwear. When the grandmother, whom Faulkner and his three brothers called Damuddy, died, the children were sent away from home so that the house could be fumigated. To Faulkner's memory of this event he added an imaginary sister, "the daughter of his mind," Caddy, who had first appeared in a story called "Twilight" before reappearing as the pivotal character of this novel. "I loved her so much," he said, that "I couldn't decide to give her life just for the duration of a short story. She deserved more than that. So my novel was created, almost in spite of myself." In Faulkner's novel we observe four children come of age amidst the decay and dissolution of their family. His sense of it began, Faulkner recalled, with "a brother and a sister splashing one another in the brook" when they have been sent away to play during the funeral of a grandmother they call Damuddy. As Caddy clambers up a tree to observe the funeral inside the house, her brothers see her muddy drawers from below. From this sequence Faulkner got several things: his sense of the brook that was sweeping Caddy away from her brothers; his sense that the girl who had the courage to climb the tree and ponder the mystery of death would also find the courage to face change and loss; and his sense that her brothers, who had waited below, would respond to loss differently, with incomprehension, despair, and rage. At this stage, Caddy, the figure of imagination added to remembered experience, had not emerged as a character. However, she seemed to offer the comfort and tenderness elsewhere unavailable from the family, and her brothers' needs for these, frustrated by their parents, could be met by her. Thus, Faulkner said, "the character of [the] sister began to emerge." Whereas readers are justifiably impressed by the technical brilliance of Faulkner's novel, they are apt to forget how simple and moving is the basic story that grew from temporal experience charged with the power of imagination.[61]

The shrine of place is where you have your roots, where you stand, your base of reference that provides validity in the raw material of writing. Fiction especially is bound up in the local, the "real" environment, the present, ordinary day-to-day of human experience. As Eudora Welty says, "The moment the place in which the novel happens is accepted as true, through it will begin to glow, in a kind of recognizable glory, the feeling and thought that inhabited the novel in the author's head and animated the whole of his work." Place, she contends, helps to make characters real and believable. "[T]he likeliest character has first to be enclosed inside the bounds of even greater likelihood," because so confined he is "set to scale in his proper world to know his size."[62] If the gods that abide in and speak from the shrine of time withhold their secrets, the shrine of place will help to focus the feeling and meaning that permeate your personal life. A world steadily visible from its outside meets our requirements for belief, then liberates the imagination to create an environment of freedom for such otherwise incredible characters as Don Quixote, Huckleberry Finn, and Lolita.

Denis Donoghue, until recently Henry James Professor of English, Irish, and American Literature at New York University and one of the foremost literary critics in the United States, is author of *The Sovereign Ghost: Studies in Imagination*. What he has to say about the imagination and those theorists who belittle or deny its importance should be required reading for anyone with a literary vocation. He is my guide in the following observations.

Nowadays some theorists of language deny the importance, even the existence, of imagination. They maintain we are more the slaves than the masters of our language, that the creative spirit is not the source of literary events but a sort of bureaucratic set that discloses predetermined social and political codes. Claiming to apply a scientific model to our mental transactions, these theorists would deny to imaginative writing the possibility of creation, freedom, play, and pleasure. Or they would denigrate the worth of these by making imagination a self-indulgence of the private life. To them, "mind" means rational consciousness, so they complain that imagination, unlike "mind," is irresponsible and impractical, doesn't improve access to technological information, doesn't increase our control over a world made dangerous by technology. Because imaginative writing fares badly in the marketplace, they argue that it is undemocratic!

But there is no inevitable quarrel between mind and imagination. Mind is not limited to purely conscious events. It includes the intuitive, the non-rational, the unconscious. Indeed, imagination is superior to "mind" that is *only* rational consciousness. Imagination might conceive of a woman's beauty as a drop of pure mountain water, but a Chinese poet who made exactly that comparison was sentenced to prison because he was supposed, when thinking of water, to think of hydroelectric plants. Luckily, as Donoghue has brilliantly argued, imagination is not committed to categories. *With freedom its cardinal virtue, imagination is the only force able to accommodate and to cope with the vast chaos of events constituting the occasions of our experience.* When a writer brings feeling to the condition of form, imagination makes experience truly known. Imagination discerns the hidden connections of things and promises an incorporating fiction, where true, universal democracy lies, immune to time and, particularly, to the ideologies that are spurious myths manufactured to control the world.[63]

In America, the imagination is engaged with forces it cannot hope to defeat, forces such as technology, big business, the military-industrial complex, advertising, public education, professional football, politicized evangelism, teachers, parents, and other organized crimes. These forces are inhospitable to imagination, which at its happiest would find real substance in the world of history and society.

This is where revolt comes in. The imagination at work in many major books of American literature seeks to expand human consciousness by revolting against the social forces that otherwise dominate American realities. Emerson, Thoreau, Hawthorne, Melville, Whitman, Mark Twain, Henry Adams, Henry James, Scott Fitzgerald, T.S. Eliot, Faulkner, Frank Waters and many other American writers try through style and structure to free themselves and their heroes from historical systems. Works like *Moby-Dick*, *Huckleberry Finn*, and *The Ambassadors* are "designed to make the reader feel that his ordinary world has been acknowledged, even exhaustively, only to be dispensed with as a source of moral or psychological standards."[64] Now, earlier, I admitted a degree of validity to stories set in outer space. One is letting go of ordinary realities—family, society, the past, even our planet—and one is letting one's characters exist in some seemingly free, natural state of the true inner self. But revolt against the difficulties of reality requires, not evasion, but confrontation of them. The hostile forces that would destroy what you love must be accorded full room in your fictions in order for the hostility to be felt as a demonic power which forbids individual fulfillment. It is only within the massed phenomena of social and economic structures that one can see the hero at all. So, sponsored by the revolt of the imagination, part of our task as writers is to provoke the hostile forces into yielding their shabbiness and inhumanity. The provocation may then have some effect upon society, redirecting the confined consciousness of the reader toward ideals of a valid culture.

Let us nevertheless remain aware of the price of revolt. Reality ultimately defeats the hero, whose success is inward and invisible. Huck Finn and Jim must abandon the idyll of the raft and return to a society based upon the conventions of slavery. Isaac McCaslin, the hero of Faulkner's *The Bear*, rejects his historical and economic inheritance, his corrupt family, and the plantation he is to inherit. This relinquishment of his inheritance allows Isaac to achieve an original, freed relationship to humanity and to the land. But his choice necessitates a lonely, sexless, childless life. In Isaac McCaslin's revolt against possessions of any kind and in his consequent self-dispossession of personal happiness, we recognize the characteristic career of many American heroes and heroines.

When you pay close attention to your experience of time and place, the mind's essential power surpasses experience and expands into a created world, the poem or story, wherein we see our real world as if for the first time. And in America, that real world is apt to be felt as preexisting organizations of power, against which the imagination revolts, producing works that demonstrate a turbulent, agitated desire to make a place for freedom and to stabilize certain feelings and values of the individual self that have been and continue to be diminished by a technological, urbanized, materialistic civilization. The fire within us succeeds on its own terms in the face of apparent defeat.

CHAPTER 6
The Last Postage Stamp

The literary practice of synecdochism as found in the novels of William Faulkner is the theme of Jay Parini's biography, *One Matchless Time* (2004). Faulkner, he writes, "took his own family history as synecdochal, standing in for the history of the South, with the South standing in for the history of the nation as a whole."[65] Yoknapatawpha County, Faulkner's invented region, is not simply a reproduction of Lafayette County, Mississippi, in a documentary fashion. It is an imaginative re-creation of that material. The sense of place in Faulkner's life and work is "a spiritual location from which he examines a truth deeper than anything like mere locality."[66] To create his vision of our whole nation Faulkner felt that he needed only, as he often said, his "postage stamp" of place.

Nowadays the sense of place has a magnitude far greater than that of a county or a nation. It is the planet itself, the last postage stamp. Consequently, the morality of literature in World Culture has to be, in order to remain authentic, *re-moralized*. God, the Bible tells us, commanded people to be fruitful and to multiply and to subdue the earth. Such a view today sounds a death-knell for the planet. It was never an object "out there" to be subdued. When we succeed in destroying our planet, which is indeed but a postage stamp in the universe, we shall have succeeded in destroying ourselves.

Can literature help to save us from ourselves? If so, how? I think synecdochism may give writers an orientation for confronting the problem. By making a place or a person stand in for and embrace a planetary whole comprised of the Others, writers from a cosmic perspective may find access to a spiritual location from which one examines the truth of our condition.

As we have seen in Campbell's discovery in the fiction of *Tristan and Iseult* and the biography of Héloise an originative locus of World Culture, a creative mythology emerges out of individual experiences of a certain depth and import. Further, this authentic mythology of the principle of individuality makes it possible for the modern novel to appear, the dynamic interplay of Experience and Authority at its heart. In my opinion, *the novel need not swerve, in future, from this path even though unbridled liberty cannot be sustained as an ideal. Only, the individual can become a vanguard-figure on a planet-stage.* A new mythology is unfolding, not diminishing his myth-status but, on the contrary, validating and enlarging it in an hour of dread for all humankind.

A World Culture engaged in planetization would expand to include a mythology of the planet. Campbell, before he died, warned a television audience of millions of the predicament of humankind when he said, "The only mythology that is valid today is the mythology of the planet—and we don't have such a mythology."[67] A few visionaries, actively casting into the shallow waters of our civilization portentous ideas, have nevertheless in my opinion been showing us ways to influence the affairs of nations. Their perceptions may ripple out to fill our need for global commitment.

Undoubtedly, there may be for writers as many ways to deal with our predicament as there are individual voices, but at least three ways, all synechdochal, can be identified from literature, nonfiction and fiction, of the past one hundred years: the way of significant soil, the way of love, and the way of Everyman. Although the art of these ways risks condemnation as didactic, the power of implication inherent in synechdochism allows each of us space to reach our own conclusions.

The Way of Significant Soil

Writers are often obsessed with what T.S. Eliot once referred to as "significant soil." As already mentioned, Faulkner in his novels revealed the obsession. His Lafayette County became his fictional region of Yoknapatawpha County, which became a stand-in for our nation. But such imaginative re-creations may be overlooked. The regional "part" that can connote a spiritual "whole" may imprint itself on memory as *merely* regional, thus popularly remembered as an author's "country." Thomas Hardy Country, Robinson Jeffers Country, and Faulkner Country are examples. Woe to the new and unknown author who seems to intrude on these "countries." For instance, the generation of Southern writers who came on the scene after Faulkner were thought to derive their works from his even though William Styron, Flannery O'Connor, Tennessee Williams and others were not lying down on the regional tracks waiting to be run over by the Dixie Special. In general, the pejorative tag of "regionalist" tends to obscure universality in a writer's work, becoming a critical obstacle to our understanding of "significant soil" as one of the ways by means of which our imaginations may inspect, as if from an orbiting spacecraft, our small blue-white-green Birdseye pea of a planet.

William deBuys is an active conservationist who lives and writes on a small farm in northern New Mexico. His elegant and painstakingingly researched book, *A Great Aridness: Climate Change and the Future of the American Southwest* (2011), might seem from its title to be regionally confined. Certainly, the American Southwest is his significant soil:

> What I have tried to do is to paint a living portrait of a region that, for my money, has no rival in beauty, richness, or fascination. This is a love story, of sorts. I came to the South-west as a young man in 1972, and, although I spent a few years elsewhere in the early 1980s. I never really left, and certainly never wanted to. For virtually all of my adult life, the Southwest has been my home, and I have felt blessed to be its student.[68]

For all his love for the Southwest, deBuys consistently views the climate-driven challenges that confront it as a paradigm for the planet and a crying-in-the-wilderness guide to its future:

> The path ahead will not be straight. The long-term trajectory of warming and drying will be interrupted by wet spells and cold snaps, some of them spectacular. The basic physics of climate change works like this: greenhouse gases trap more of the heat that Earth would otherwise radiate back into space. The retained heat charges the atmosphere and the oceans—the main drivers of the planetary climate system—with more energy, loading them with more oomph to do the things they already do, but more powerfully than before.[69]

After presenting a detailed study of the chaos of weather in the Southwest, deBuys concludes that the region's future stands in for an entirely new geological epoch, the planetary name for which is Anthropocene:

> In 1807, a group of scientists interested in ascertaining the age of Earth and pursuing other provocative questions formed the London Geological Society. It was the world's first national organization dedicated to the earth sciences. Two centuries later, in 2008, the Society's Stratigraphy Commission, a respected voice on the classification of geologic time, delivered a portentous report to the main body. The impact of human-induced change on the planet, said the commission, "has so intensified to make our present interval comparable to major global perturbations of the geological past." As a result, "a new geological epoch, worthy of formalization, may indeed have commenced."
>
> The members of the commission were not merely alluding to the age-old human capacity to alter ecosystems, rather, they sought to draw attention to something new under the sun: a cumulative and determinative human effect on core planetary processes, primarily climate. They said the Holocene epoch, the period since the end of the last ice age and the incubator of human civilization, was now at an end. A new geologic epoch had begun. The name the commission suggested for the new epoch was already in currency in certain circles: Anthropocene—the human or human shaped epoch. The commission postulated that one might mark its onset at about the time the Society was formed, at the start of the Industrial Revolution. In the life of the planet, as well as the history of humankind, the Anthropocene constitutes a new beginning, the dawning of a new drama, and it is happening now—in the "long now" of the geologic present.[70]

One might ask, if the way of significant soil leads us, as deBuys makes clear, to recognize and identify a new epoch and to see in that "human-shaped" epoch an apocalyptic threat to civilization and our natural environment, what is now opening up for the imaginative poet, dramatist, and fiction writer? The answer to that question is, as deBuys presents it, exhilarating: he conjures up the ever-present dramatics of Shakespeare. The relevance of Shakespeare to climate change is in fact profound: climate change begets tragedy. I again quote from deBuys:

The essence of tragedy in Shakespeare's time was considered to be an essential blindness, an inability of the tragic figure to recognize the flaw in himself that causes his fall . . . Hamlet could have pulled himself together. Lear might have appraised the motives of his daughters, and himself, more shrewdly. Macbeth might have ignored his wife and Othello trusted his. The problems that exist at the level of these invented characters exist equally at the level of society. When to believe? Whether and when to act? How to put aside doing what one wants and commence doing what one must?

Notwithstanding a large cast of senatorial ideologues, right-wing bloviators, and modern-day Iago's lobbying for Big Coal and Big Oil, the protagonists in this drama are the rest of us, our collectivity, the commonwealth, including the creatures and communities of nonhuman nature.[71]

In sum, obstacles to climate change are a particularly contemporary form of blindness. When and if lunatics are running the asylum, there are enough tragic figures to lure some paranoid protagonists into fantasies of abandoning the ship of Earth and, like rats before it sinks, sending a few virile and ovulating astronauts into space in hopes they will be fruitful and multiply and subdue another speck of sidereal dust.

The categories of paralysis, "the list of mental obstacles to action on climate change," are, deBuys writes, "nearly inexhaustible."[72] It is a demoralizing list: denial, habit, impotence ("What can I do?"), ignorance, uncertainty, belief in divine intervention, mulishness, all those behaviors and more. Because they are inhibiting human behaviors and always have been, they can easily seem to be our "friends". Soon we fear to recognize these behaviors for what they are: tyrants. Perhaps more than anyone else, writers can—and should—re-moralize images of an Earth beyond tyranny.

Take Habit. The power of Habit was very well understood, Montaigne told us centuries ago, by the man who first forged the tale of a village woman who had grown used to cuddling a calf and carrying it about from the time it was born. She grew so accustomed to doing so that she was able to carry it when it became a fully-grown bull. Comparing Habit to a violent and treacherous school teacher, Montaigne continues, she gradually and stealthily slides her authoritative foot into us, "then, having by this gentle and humble beginning planted it firmly within us, helped by time she later discloses an angry tyrannous countenance, against which we are no longer allowed even to lift up our eyes."[73]

Let a writer's resolution be: *demoralization shall be re-moralization.*

Any planet-saving mythology is going to have to confront the categories of paralysis. Incredible as it seems, humans have lived for untold thousands of years without suspecting that the stars above us are hundreds of light-years away, or that the universe is formed of millions of galaxies whose distance apart runs into hundreds of light-years away, or that the contours of life stretch out millions of years behind us. Our immediate forebears nevertheless felt at ease in a space-time where stars turned around the Earth and had been doing so for fewer than 6,000 years. The conviction of historical, as opposed to spiritual, truth in scriptures more than 2,000 years old has been and still is for countless millions of people a habit. Even as the hour of planetization is sounding for all mankind, those who speak of love and brotherhood and solidarity usually reserve their pieties for an in-group or bounded community, projecting aggression outward upon other groups because it is our bull-lugging habit to divide the world up according to tribes, nations, races, religions and ideologies. Boundaries, however, no longer exist even though a self-styled "modern" individual believes that any agglomeration stifles and neutralizes the elements that compose it. Man and nature are inter-related, inter-connected. Only in countries of the blind can we continue to believe that our planet is an object to be exploited and plundered.

The Way of Love

Let us suppose there is a constantly rising tide of life with an expanding and deepening of human consciousness as its thrust. Let us suppose that we ourselves are part of vast and continuous processes and that nature demands the true union of humankind in an association that promotes instead of eliminates the differences of its separate elements. Let us suppose that heart and spirit are united as a phenomenon on a terrestrial scale.

These suppositions have already been tallied and explored by visionaries in the twentieth century, two of whom are Pierre Teilhard de Chardin, a French priest-scientist, and Frank Waters, an American novelist-philosopher.

Frank Waters said, quote:

> Today, I believe, we are beginning to experience another periodic expansion toward a psychic, universal consciousness which will

supersede our rational, terrestrial mode of thinking: leap . . . toward a new perspective inspired by a planetary imperative.[74]

Pierre Teilhard de Chardin said, quote:

> True union, the union of heart and spirit, does not enslave, nor does it neutralize the individuals which it brings together. It *super-personalizes* them . . . Imagine men awakening at last, under the influence of the ever-tightening planetary embrace, to a sense of universal solidarity based on their profound community, evolutionary in its nature and purpose. The nightmares of brutalization and mechanization which are conjured up to terrify us and prevent our advance are at once dispelled. It is not harshness or hatred, but a new kind of love, not yet experienced by man, which we must learn to look for as it is borne to us on the rising tide of planetization. (*Emphasis in original*)[75]

Born in Auvergne in 1881, Teilhard was sent to a Jesuit College at the age of ten and ordained a priest in 1912. He then embarked on a geological career, with special emphasis on paleontology, later synthesizing these studies with biology. Having spent most of his career in China, there completing the manuscript of *Le Phénomène Humain* in 1938, he returned to France in 1946 only to encounter difficulty: he was forbidden in 1948 to put forward his Professorship in the Collège de France, and in 1950 his application to publish his philosophical work was refused in Rome. At the invitation of the Wenner-Gren Foundation he moved to New York in 1951. He died there in 1955. His great work, *Le Phénomène Humain*, was published in French that year. The English translation, *The Phenomenon of Man*, appeared in 1959 with an introduction by Sir Julian Huxley who had independently envisaged human evolution and biological evolution as two phases of a single process.

According to Huxley, Teilhard had already by 1919

> reached a point where the entire phenomenal universe, including man, was revealed as a process of evolution, and he found himself impelled to build up a generalized theory of philosophy of evolutionary process which could take account of human history and human personality as well as of biology and from which one could draw conclusions as to the future evolution of man on earth.[76]

It was imperative for Teilhard, Huxley continues, "to try to reconcile Christian theology with this evolutionary philosophy, to relate the facts of religious experience to those of natural science."[77]

Key terms in Teilhard's philosophy are *emergence* and *convergence*. Waters uses a single term, *Emergence*, to convey both concepts. In summarizing the meaning of these terms, beginning with Teilhard's, I draw upon language from both writers.

For Teilhard, *emergence* denotes the increasingly elaborate organization of life in its passage from the sub-atomic units to atoms, from atoms to inorganic and then to organic molecules, thence to the first sub-cellular units or self-replicating assemblages of molecules, then to cells, to multi-cellular individuals, to cephalized metazoa with brains, to primitive man, and now to civilized societies. Emergence also denotes an original imprisonment in the matter of earth of a certain mass of elementary consciousness. Consciousness, too, has been in process. It leaped forward with cephalization, that is, the differentiation of the head as the dominant guiding region of the body.

The emergence of human beings with their power of reflective thought—a consciousness no longer merely knowing but knowing itself—has given them in a flash the capacity to raise themselves to a new sphere of increased awareness and thus to a future on the planet.

First, then, man alone constitutes the last-born, the freshest, and the most complicated of all the successive layers of life. Second, man's augmenting consciousness is nothing less than the substance and heart of life in process of evolution. Third, the direction of life, whatever "conservatives" say, is irreversible. The road ahead is not only open to individual fulfillment, but also, as regards the choices and responsibilities of our activity, open to the unanimous construction of a spirit of the Earth.

For Teilhard *convergence* denotes the tendency of humankind during its evolution to incorporate in an organized and unified pattern the fragmentations that have enervated the progress of other species. Convergence has prevented humankind from diverging into separated species even though there is differentiation in races and cultures. In natural fact it is convergence that has led to an accelerating process of psychological union of the whole human species into a single inter-thinking group. Especially in our own times with the dramatic increase of human numbers, convergence necessitates that kind of integrated mental activity that can guide our species to higher levels—integration of the self with the outer world of men and nature, and integration of the separate elements of the self with each other.

The plurality of individual reflections grouping themselves together in a mega-synthesis is a grand and enabling vision. Under the influence of a supremely autonomous focus of unanimity the more Other we become in conjunction, the more depth we have as parts of an organized whole, although we must be on our guard to prevent collective organization which might—and already has in totalitarian regimes—lower and enslave consciousness. Human beings must be united by what is deepest in themselves into a sort of super-consciousness, by love, not by forced coalescence. We must come together inwardly and in entire freedom. As a corollary to this proposition, we must recognize that egocentricity is against nature, a blind alley.

> The life-giving coming together of mankind . . . links those who love in bonds that unite but do not confound, causing them to discover in their mutual contact an exaltation, capable incomparably more than any arrogance of solitude, of arousing in the heart of their being all that they possess of uniqueness and creative power.[78]

Recognition or contemplation of the truth has been a staple of plot construction at least since Aristotle wrote the *Poetics* in the fourth century B.C. as an empirical guide to understanding what a poet is aiming at and how he puts his play or poem (and for us a novel) together. Poets, Aristotle says, "imitate action," and by "action" he means not physical activity but a movement-of-spirit, the working out of a motive to its end. After passing through unforeseeable contingencies, human actions, at the end, in the light of hindsight, are perceived and illuminated. "Recognition," Aristotle writes, ". . . is a change from ignorance to knowledge."[79]

Clearly, what Teilhard is aiming at in his sense of evolution as destiny and of that ultimate destiny as love is to offer a *way*, one that can be dramatized to move the individual spirit with its augmenting consciousness to recognition of an all-embracing spirit of the Earth.

The Way of Everyman

The Phenomenon of Man, germinating in 1919, written in 1938, and published in English in 1959, could not have exercised an influence on Waters' philosophy of *Emergence* as it first achieved clarity in *The Man Who Killed the Deer*, his novel written in 1941 and published in 1942. Working independently and reaching similar conclusions, Teilhard and Waters give us a glimpse of our last postage stamp, the planet, having to offer us, as it were, a mythology to live by. Waters, unlike Teilhard, is drawn to primal myths about a Goddess Mother and Mother Earth, but, like Teilhard, he was scientifically trained and in a quest to synthesize ancient religion and modern science to create a fresh spirit.

Waters apperceived an Ultimate Reality underlying all forms and man-ifesting itself in us as we are in it. Although Waters is in general agreement with Teilhard about evolutionary process, particularly with respect to an enlargement of consciousness in humanity, he does not project our inward coming together as a specifically Christian, let alone Utopian, future. For him, planetization is not to be sought after by acts of individual or collective will. The ego obstructs such seeking. Integration is already here, already inherent. *We are already the Other.* Man is essentially related to, merged with, or em-bodied with all living entities, including humankind. As he writes in *Mexico Mystique*:

> In the supreme law governing both external and internal realities, there seems to be a factor of cohesiveness that links in one great process the evolving life of every microscopic cell and giant star. Planets, animals, man, the Earth itself, may be but microcosmic reflections of that macrocosmic life which also informs all planets in our solar system and the farthest galaxies in a universe too great to be conceived by the human mind. All are embodied in the same cosmic process of the whole.[80]

For Waters, *Emergence* incorporates from natural science the Teilhardian concepts of emergence and convergence and from religion the concept of a universe embodied in a supreme power. Using different approaches, Waters through psychology, Teilhard through biology, both envisage a new world of the mind. Waters's *Emergence* represents a stage of human consciousness that reconciles the duality of reason and instinct and supersedes these in a numi-nous plane, the effulgence of an immanent power that relates the inner world of man to the living universe, itself composed of expanding psychic as well as the physical energies. From this perspective, which is, above all, evolution-ary, the long journey of humankind has been through successive states of ever-expanding consciousness. From complete polarization to the instinctive or unconscious mentation man has emerged to his present state of rational consciousness and must not surrender this advantage over the other forms of life or sink back into the unconscious. Excessively rationalistic modern man, however, has become alienated from the source of life. Suffering a loss of relationship to nature and to humankind, he has reached a spiritual and ethical dead end. Now his task is to live in harmonious relationship with all the emergent life forces. Once he recognizes on the plane of increased awareness his indebtedness to these forces and his responsibility for them, his taking responsibility for the planet can no longer be postponed.

Human conscience, though it may be local and tribal in orientation and enforcement, serves all humanity in World Culture because conscience pulls individuals back from ego-centeredness into harmonic relationships at all levels, rippling out from family to tribe to society, to all peoples, to all living things and to the cosmos.

Emergence is allegorized in Waters's novel *The Man Who Killed the Deer*. The protagonist's actions and thoughts resemble those of a man possessed by a primary illusion that he is in control of his fate. Then the powers of conscience and intuition appear to him in the form of a spirit-deer, whereupon he loses his illusion by recognizing his obligation to the dictates of the unconscious and emerges to a state of increased awareness. There is a culminating character to this allegory: the protagonist experiences final moments of illumination.

The story of the protagonist, who is a Native American, stands in for the story of humankind on Earth as a whole.

For many readers *The Man Who Killed the Deer* seems a treatise in cultural anthropology: a hero departs from Anglo culture and returns to the Indian blanket. But is *Deer* such a story? Is it about an "individual" who submerges himself in the "collective"? In our culture this is a negative outcome. We have no patience with individuals who surrender their freedom, especially when we distort the word "freedom" to mean a lack of requirement. Close analysis of the story, as I've indicated, reveals that the hero, by returning figuratively to the Cosmic Mother, the feminine power of the unconscious, exemplifies a vision that is not culture-specific but universal. Far from abandoning the *modern* world, he is emblematic of the truly free, non-alienated, modern individual who has recovered the richness and the wonder and the mystery of life. *Deer*, while remaining faithful to the form of Indian life, reveals to our non-collective mind-set a substance at the heart of contemporary ethics, for the ethic of fullness demands an organic relationship whereby an individual is dependent on the existence of all other persons and of all living things, *"breathing mountains, the living stones, each blade of grass, the clouds, the rain, each star, the beasts, the birds, and the invisible spirits of the air"* and *"universal brotherhood."*[81] The metonymical figure or symbol for all life is in this novel the deer.

To liberate his allegorical hero, Martiniano, into the substance of Indian life, Waters shows that a strong sense of tribal unity has been achieved and at the same time articulates feelings productive of a complex, permanent attitude which governs all individual lives once it is recognized. In the light of the mystery of life we may perceive our own role in the cosmic plan and return to psychic balance and right attitudes. *The Man Who Killed the Deer* is an "Everyman" novel, one in which salvation is at stake.

The consonance between objective facts and their moral or psychological counterparts provides the basis for an allegory. As correspondences evolve within the story, the dominant idea begins to be revealed through accretion of meanings. Martiniano progresses through successive states of mind until his relationship to the symbolic deer grows. When he is not in harmony with it, an ironic discrepancy between symbol and state of mind invalidates authenticity. Like as not, he will seek substitutes for the reality as yet unilluminated for him. For example, because Christians in the Middle Ages were fond of listening to homilies on people's futile efforts to find a substitute for salvation, *Everyman* (ca. 1485) presents an allegory of a person who accepts all the substitutes society offers but finds himself suddenly confronted with the reality of death. Similarly, Martiniano defies the pueblo, seeks legal redress for his grievances, looks for a faith in marriage and then in peyote, wants, like Captain Ahab, vengeance against an animal, and works up a savior complex, only to be haunted and "defeated" by the spirit-deer, with which he must finally learn to live, in order to be "saved," to emerge, to be authentic—in effect to become the representative figure for all of us who are living on the planet now and for those who live on it in future.

From the very beginning of *Deer*, Waters distinguishes two views of nature, the one materialistic, the other sacred. When Martiniano kills a deer out of season, he violates man-made law and must pay a fine. To elders at the pueblo, however, he has, in failing to show proper reverence for the slain deer, violated the natural order. What is being desiderated is an idea of order that makes for balance, health, harmony and peace. Edwin Honig asserts that in allegory the irrational is "given an authentic, undiminished force which otherwise—according to law, custom, dogma—would be distorted or obscured."[82]

The constant layering of meaning in allegory proves to be decisive in creating the whole effect a literary work can have upon us. In a society such as our own, one that favors the patriarchal principle and harnesses the idea of freedom to rational consciousness and the idea of God to a one-sided power of goodness and love—even as the threat of planetary destruction hangs over us like the sword of Damocles—an archetypal vision on the order of *The Man Who Killed the Deer* has the value of myth. Everything opens out in back to eternity, to the structuring laws and forces interior to the earthly being that is man, here and now. The concept of a coming world of consciousness refers to a view of reality in which individual actions combine into something more organized, our power for embracing the totality of Earth. We could call this power a new kind of love.

World Culture, with its centering of awe and wonder in the human heart, is in crisis. Now to celebrate the "individual" in literature, we must take into account that we are all in the same boat.

CHAPTER 7

Breath of Life

The descent of the inspirational self on the writer as his mind moves over his materials enables him to create. We know that memory dredges up to the surface of consciousness lost time and sources in reading. Some materials, perhaps slumbering since infancy and perhaps archetypal, have to be found, while other materials are kept waiting for the opportune time for the poem or story. We nevertheless hardly know precisely and in advance when imagination will take over. The recalcitrance of the materials has to be overcome before life is breathed into them.

A fundamental way for meeting obstacles is to keep on writing until "something" happens. That, for poets as well as for story writers, is what I call the way of the golden nugget, the image that is going to support you for the long endeavor. If you have the fire within, which is synonymous with initiative, drive, intuition and instinct, you'll probably have the perseverance to find the magical image, the nugget of gold. Fool's gold, formulaic sentimentalist stuff, may deceive you into becoming temporarily enriched, but that golden image is your eureka.

Consider the sluice operation.

That summer of 1950 when war broke out in Korea and I declined the offer of a newspaper job in Alaska, I met a rich man who epitomized the risk-taking, entrepreneurial spirit, one I could admire as long as I didn't call to mind the masses of workers he probably trampled and tossed aside like Kleenex. The rich man made his first fortune in fishing, then lost everything, made his second fortune in timbering, then lost everything again. He was now making a third fortune in gold mining. At the age of seventy-five he had a mine in British Columbia. As long as he could make his profit, he didn't care about camels that can't pass through the eye of a needle. When he offered to let me accompany him and his wife for an inspection tour of his mine, I accepted the invitation immediately. He seemed to a naïve college student kind, and I wanted adventure. He promised I could see the aurora borealis and mosquitoes big as elephants. As for the mine, I, a romantic of sorts, expected to find a crew of Forty-Niners panning for gold in a creek full of dead men's bones.

We set out early one morning from Seattle in the rich man's Cadillac. Once we crossed the border into Canada, with him behind the wheel, he kept the speedometer above his age, saving a measly 75 mph for curves on the unpaved shelf roads without guard rails. Below us the Fraser River gleamed in the sun. As I was having the mother of conniptions, I figured that one heedlessly death-defying old man's twitch on the steering wheel and we would be airborne for the heavenly reward of a 1000-foot plunge into the river. He slowed down once. We were approaching a hairpin curve at the center of which a sign had been thoughtfully planted. It read, "Prepare to Meet Thy God." Evidently, he felt prepared. We somehow arrived at the mining camp at dusk, our cabins perched above a black lake. I asked the rich man a sensible question, black lakes back East usually being full of spilled oil.

"Sir," I asked, "how come the lake yonder is so black?"

The question surprised him. I think he had thought until then that I, being a Yale man and all, was intelligent. "Son," he said after a long pause, punctuated by a sigh of resignation, "them's salmon. Spawning."

Apparently, he wasn't tall-taleing me. The lake, large and deep as the Yale Bowl, had a brood of several millions of fish, almost motionless in a kind of perpetual séance.

We toured the "mine" next day. Miles from the lake there were tractors scooping up tons of gravel and dumping it in waiting trucks. Rattling and groaning, the trucks came and dumped the gravel into a channel of pumped-in water moving at the speed of a flash flood in a "sluice," a long, inclined trough that makes possible the agitation and washing needed to separate gold ore from gravel. Like an enormous guitar with frets on the neck, each of them about a foot high, the sluice I saw was about a hundred yards in length, beginning at the top of a hill and, at the bottom, poking into the lake.

At five o'clock a bunch of bindle stiffs lumbered down muddy slopes, pausing at frets to collect nuggets snagged by them.

That was the sluice operation. By analogy it is an *imagination operation*: keep on dumping the piles of subject matter, the research, the notebooks, the inchoate drafts and false starts, until you dig out from them the golden image descending, had you not overlooked it, with breath of life.

It will suffice to enrich you with an exuberance unknown to my host in British Columbia who told me with a disgruntled look at the end of our visit, "I didn't break even. I'm making only 10,000 bucks a day." Since affluence already entitled him to salvation, he was not plagued by feelings of guilt, inadequacy, or sin and could look forward to an afterlife resembling a suburb in Seattle.

A brief example I can attest to. For several years I explored the possibility of writing a novel about the history of coalmining wars in Colorado, these culminating in the Ludlow Massacre of 20 April 1914. In addition to that history I investigated stories of immigrants who would have become miners, and stories of John D. Rockefeller, Jr., who had owned the mines in Colorado. I collected all the information I could about mining of coal, the United Mine Workers of America, company towns and other subjects. After gathering these materials, I believed I was ready to write my novel based upon them. I was wrong. After many an attempt to make a story in which historical characters would come alive, all the pre-writing I had produced was rehashed history. The "characters" weren't characters at all in the genuinely fictional sense. At best, they were impersonations of the dead, puppets on a string, preconceived and stillborn. I was discouraged. The closest I had ever really come to a coal mine was, after all, a canary in a cage at a pet store.

Then one day it happened. I was digging through my mountain of verbal tundra and suddenly found, half buried in the frozen sub-soil, the following sentence:

> After a while this train, chugging and wheezing like an asthmatic giant punching himself in the gut, loomed above me, then rumbled past where I lay, leaving a diminishing *clickitty rickitty clickitty rackitty*.

Unprepossessing, that sentence is now buried again on the 28th page of *The Door of the Sad People*. Its immediate impact on me was electrifying. Within seconds I "received" from the imagination operation the image of a boy in the freight car of a train, its locomotive straining to make the grade on a hill, altitude 7,500 feet, in southern Colorado in 1903. He had been kidnapped and was being guarded by Pinkerton detectives who, presently, would throw him out of the car and into the desert. There, hours later, he would be rescued by a rancher, a veteran of the Philippines War who was secretly serving as a labor organizer for miners. In short, I had within a few seconds discovered enough golden imagery to give me close to half of all I would need to free a novel from the clutches of historical material.

Here's another example of imagination operation, something Mac Hyman said to me. Although I interpret what he said in order to support my thesis, I believe the anecdote to be close enough in reality to what I have to say about it as to merit disclosure.

When Mac was my father's writing student at Duke after the Second World War, I was away at school and didn't know him, nor did I meet him until March 1955 when *No Time for Sergeants* was appearing on TV. Mac was nervously elated by his sudden fame. In his Georgia accent he referred to his producer, Shakespearean actor Maurice Evans, as "MO-reese." It was if they had guns and grits in common. He liked the actor Andy Griffith personally but hated the way the show's star was converting the character of Will into what Mac called a "moron."

Mac was born in 1923 in the small town of Cordele in Georgia. He entered the Army Air Corps in the spring of 1943 and the following year received his commission as a photo-navigator. Soon thereafter he was overseas in the South Pacific, based in Guam, and in 1945 it was his plane that flew over Hiroshima to take the reconnaissance photographs the day after the atomic bomb was dropped. In the next eighteen years he wrote two novels, publishing *Sergeants* in his lifetime, and Bill Styron, Max Steele, and Peter Matthiessen at *The Paris Review* published one brilliant short story, "The Hundredth Centennial." Posthumously his letters were published by my father. I'll quote from Max Steele's "Introduction" to that book:

> In 1954 he publishes a book, No Time for Sergeants, and now his life becomes the dream life of many young men. He has a successful book, a phenomenal best-seller, that is made into a profitable play and movie. He has money and a great deal of it, enough that with care he probably will never have to work another day in his life.

He has a beautiful wife, two daughters, and in 1955 a son. He has a hometown where he is known . . . and where he is respected by all men as a good hunter, fisherman, swimmer, surf boarder, card player, pool player, and golfer. In short, in the expression of that day, "he has it made."

Soon he has a colonial house appropriately furnished, a beach house in Florida with a swimming pool, a cabin cruiser in which, with friends, he maneuvers the inland waterway from St. Augustine to Miami. He buys cars, large and automatic and pneumatic and air-conditioned for his family; small ones fast and perfectly adaptable to his own small frame and quick, nervous, deadly accurate reflexes. He has part-interest in a gun shop and in a skeet range. When necessary—and since he cannot be a writer in Cordele because he cannot accept the role there—he has, to satisfy the restlessness brought on by the desire to write, an apartment, or sometimes a room, in New York, or a country house on Long Island, or a place in Connecticut, and when he wants to go to try to write on the West Coast he takes a house there near the Pacific Ocean. He can go wherever he pleases, to Europe with his wife, for instance, or to Greece alone or with friends; and he can buy whatever he wants. He is, by ordinary standards in this country, a fortunate man. And in 1963, at the age of forty, he dies of a heart attack.[83]

In September 1955 Mac used my apartment in New York as a daytime studio where he could write without distractions. He had plenty of those to bother him. *No Time for Sergeants* was running on Broadway, it seemed, forever, and Warner Brothers was talking movie contracts. Although he spent nights at his sister's nearby apartment, his wife and kids were back home in Georgia. In a sense he compensated for loneliness by having for company at the end of a day's writing someone he rather flabbergastingly regarded as a fellow creative writer. While I was away all-day teaching in a private elementary school, Mac, seated before his typewriter, was daily turning out and reading aloud to me twenty pages of solid, Mark-Twainish prose. He didn't think well of it.

One afternoon he looked at me in despair and said, "All I want to write is tragedy, but all they," meaning publishers and producers, "want me to write is comedy." While a million people were reading or viewing *Sergeants* and laughing until they cried, Mac wanted them to perceive that he had told the story of a country boy who had been in the military and was trying to find his way back to humanity! Something he said on another afternoon has significance for imaginative writers. Home so exhausted from teaching grammar and arithmetic to ten-year-old extra-terrestrials I could have flopped on my bed in the attitude of the Crucifixion, I found Mac bubbling over with excitement. "If I get the names right," he exclaimed, "I get fifty percent of the story!" For Mac the suddenly appearing names of characters were the breath of life, a magic whereby truly imaginative fiction triumphed over anxieties about judgments earthly and otherwise.

The text of an author's work is usually the place to begin a literary investigation—what the words mean, what the style conveys. Textual criticism becomes an indispensable method which in the light shed by historical data can make authors living or dead a felt presence.

Who was Shakespeare? A William Shakespeare existed all right. He was an actor and stage manager from Stratford who, suddenly affluent, purchased a coat of arms and bequeathed to a daughter, apparently with no ill feelings— or no sense of irony—his "second-best bed." But was this bourgeois gentleman the world's greatest poet? Many a playgoer couldn't care less who wrote the plays. The Bard of Stratford will do, and the Bard presides over a billion-dollar industry. Still, who really breathed life into the materials of those poems and plays? There has long been a disconnection between the banal biography of the Bard and the sublime wording of his works. True, it seems snobbish to dismiss that Bard from realms of gold, but he must in fact be dismissed. There are mounds of evidence in favor of another Elizabethan whose biography is exceedingly well-known and persuasively linked to his texts. The Bard simply could not have been the courtier, the scholar, the actor and the true poet who is everywhere in those texts.

Scholars have chuckled about the Bard's ignorance of geography, in particular his stage direction in *The Winter's Tale* about "the seacoast of Bohemia." Since many scholars are comfortable in believing Bohemia never had a seacoast, they feel satisfied that they, for once, know more than the dear provincial chap who blotted his copybook.

Edward de Vere traveled abroad and had intimate knowledge, evinced in numerous plays, of Italy and of the Adriatic down the Illyrian (now Croatian) coastline. In 1575 he wished to visit the Ottoman-occupied lands to the east of Italy. He took a 1100-mile, 15-day voyage down that very coastline to Athens. His biographer describes an interesting aspect of the voyage:

> Upon leaving Venetian waters, within the first forty-eight hours under sail, the galley would have passed along a thirty-five-mile stretch of Hungarian coastline, the seafaring end of a kingdom then ruled by Rudolf II, king of Bohemia. This Bohemian corridor was a mere finger of land squeezed between the Holy Roman and Ottoman Empires. And yet, between 1575 and 1609, the king of Bohemia and Hungary did in fact command a small parcel of seacoast. *The Winter's Tale* acknowledges this little-known fact of Central European history by setting several scenes on the "seacoast of Bohemia."[85]

The man who was "Shakespeare" was in all probability Edward de Vere, Earl of Oxford. Such a small detail establishes nothing persuasive by itself. Add to it, however, hundreds of similar details, and little doubt remains about authorship of the poems and plays of "Shakespeare." To be fair to bardolaters, I admit that absolute proof is still wanting.

Here's another piece of evidence from Mark Anderson's *"Shakespeare" by Another Name: The Life of Edward de Vere, Earl of Oxford, The Man Who Was Shakespeare.*

In 1562 a twelve-year-old boy who had just lost his father became a ward of the English crown. Because he was predestined for the life of an aristocrat close to affairs of the court, his education had to be extensive and austere. He was sent to live in the household of Sir William Cecil, First Baron Burghley, chief secretary of state to Queen Elizabeth I and the most powerful man in England. Cecil had a great library, one that boasted some 1700 titles and 250 manuscripts, to all of which the boy, an omnivorous reader under the tutorship of Laurence Nowell, a famed expert in Anglo-Saxon, had access. Sometime in 1563, the same year Nowell was tutoring the now thirteen-year-old boy, Nowell signed his name in a volume of manuscripts containing the only known copy of *Beowulf.* The boy almost certainly read it or had it read to him.

For centuries scholars have been puzzled over resemblances between *Beowulf* and *Hamlet.* How could William Shakespeare of Stratford manage to read a unique Anglo-Saxon manuscript in Cecil House? The resemblances between the two literary works were simply inexplicable. Anderson clarifies the matter:

> *Beowulf* was as inaccessible as the crown jewels to anyone outside of Cecil House. With an author whose childhood education

would have exposed him to *Beowulf*, the ancient poem's influence on Shakespeare becomes not inexplicable but rather expected . . . Once Hamlet kills his uncle Claudius, Shakespeare stops following "Amleth" and starts following *Beowulf*. It is Beowulf who fights the mortal duel with poison and sword; it is Beowulf who turns to his loyal comrade (Wiglaf in *Beowulf*; Horatio in *Hamlet*) to recite a dying appeal to carry his name and cause forward; and it is *Beowulf* that carries on after its hero's death to dramatize a succession struggle for the throne brought on by an invading foreign nation.[86]

A fog lifts. The boy who at the age of twelve lost his father is very likely creator of the character Hamlet who mourns the loss of his own father. The guardian, Sir William Cecil, is also very likely Polonius, the dithering busybody whose job it is to sniff out treason.

Here, though the biographical connections of de Vere to *Hamlet* are fascinating, I shall have to limit examples to the transmission of *Beowulf* to the play. Upon reaching maturity the boy who read *Beowulf* or had it read to him remembered the manuscript and found what he needed for the conclusion of *Hamlet*. From this singular source material, the playwright's imagination took over. That the transmission actually took place, elevating matter to magic, is highly probable.

I confess I'm particularly fond of writers who remember with pride and humility their struggles. One of them is Herman Melville. The artist's struggle he likens in his poem "Art" to the biblical tale of Jacob's wrestling with divinity:

> *In placid hours well-pleased we dream*
> *Of many a brave unbodied scheme.*
> *But form to lend, pulsed life create,*
> *What unlike things must meet and mate:*
> *A flame to melt—a wind to freeze;*
> *Sad patience—joyous energies;*
> *Humility—yet pride and scorn;*
> *Instinct and study; love and hate;*
> *Audacity—reverence. These must mate,*
> *And fuse with Jacob's mystic heart,*
> *To wrestle with the angel—Art.*[87]

To create "pulsed life" depends upon the fire within.

The story of Jacob came also to the mind of Conrad as he recalled his own struggles:

> All I know, is that, for twenty months, neglecting the common joys of life that fall to the lot of the humblest on this earth, I had, like the prophet of old, "*wrestled with the Lord*" for my creation, for the headlands of the coast, for the darkness of the Placid Gulf, the light of the snows, the clouds on the sky, and for the *breath of life* that had to be blown into the shapes of men and women, of Latin and Saxon, of Jew and Gentile. These are, perhaps, strong words, but it is difficult to characterize otherwise the intimacy and the strain of a creative effort in which mind and will and conscience are engaged to the full, hour after hour, day after day, away from the world, and to the exclusion of all that makes life really lovable and gentle—something for which a material parallel can only be found in the everlasting somber stress of the westward winter passage around Cape Horn. For that too is the *wrestling of men with the might of their creator*, in a great isolation from the world, without the amenities and consolations of life, a lonely struggle under a sense of over-matched littleness, for no reward that could be adequate, but for mere winning of a longitude. Yet a certain longitude, once won, cannot be disputed. (*Emphasis added*)[88]

The lonely struggle can take its toll on writers if the recalcitrance of the materials doesn't yield itself in a satisfactory manner to imagination. But the elation of inspiration, in general usage the prompting of the mind in a creative act, is not to be gainsaid. Inspiration is literally a "breathing into." To my way of thinking, the word *inspiration* links up with *compassion*, literally to "suffer with," and *empathy*, literally "feeling with." An inspired writer has the power of mentally identifying with, and so fully comprehending, a person or object of contemplation. The capacity for compassion and empathy is what makes us fully human.

It is fashionable, I suppose, to scoff at source studies in literature. I do not wish to pick a quarrel with Harold Bloom, the eminent aesthetician, as he stands every chance of winning in a field of study made ferocious since Aristotle. Still, I believe that his calling "mere source study" little more than "a benign process" can be challenged.[89] Inspiration, compassion, and empathy, after all, are aspects of a dynamic process, an infectious process, if you will, and not all infections are benign. Source studies in literature give us a glimpse of the interconnectedness of mind and matter. If that isn't significant—scientifically significant in quantum physics—we may well deserve to populate the world with formulaic sentimentalists. As James Baldwin reminded us, "Sentimentality, the ostentatious parading of excessive and spurious emotion, is a mark of dishonesty, the inability to feel. The wet eyes of the sentimentalist betray his aversion to experience, his fear of life, his arid heart, and it is always, therefore, the signal of secret and violent inhumanity, the mask of cruelty."[90]

Source studies, I admit, are often "academic" in a pejorative sense, especially if "source" is inflated into "influence." Dante influenced T.S. Eliot. Faulkner influenced García-Márquez. Walt Whitman influenced Pablo Neruda. Shakespeare influenced everybody. If you're trained to glorify trends, traditions, pigeon holes and canonizations, or fall into a Marxian rabbit hole of linguistics and deconstruction, some investigative scholars may doubt if you really know how to order a cup of coffee. The creative writer, like the literary scholar, may carry the major (and not-so-major) writers around with him by way of internalization and may need them for his wrestling with the angel. I would encourage any student of English literature to read John Livingston Lowes's book on Samuel Taylor Coleridge's sources, *The Road to Xanadu: A Study of the Ways of the Imagination* (1927). It took him an entire book to track down those sources for "The Rime of the Ancient Mariner" and "Kubla Khan," and then to connect this material's very words and contexts to the poems. By showing mental processes and masses of facts pointing to a maze of baffling inconsistencies toward a magical flash of vision constituting something like the zenith of a creative spirit, Lowes fathomed the depths of mentation from which burst some of the most unforgettable lines in English poetry. Coleridge often adapted passages from other writers with little to no acknowledgement after his spasms of intense effort, thus leaving clues to what he had been reading. Transforming reading material, Lowes shows, is not like assembling a jigsaw puzzle in Sherlock Holmesian fashion. It is something else entirely: vision. I shall return to Coleridge presently.[91]

Norman Sherry's *Conrad's Western World* (1971) demonstrates that materials created whole cloth outside of personal experience may yield to a novelist his plot, theme, and various characters. I touched on this phenomenon when I discussed how the image of a train liberated me from a small library of sources in my reading. Sherry makes it axiomatic that largeness of vision is a critical achievement superior to ordinary memories. The resuscitating of memories about the Belgian Congo certainly gives *Heart of Darkness* (1899) matter that Conrad could develop, but *Nostromo* (1904), developed out of matter mainly derived from reading and from yarns told him by friends, is, Sherry argues, the greater achievement. Conrad asserted in his "Author's Note" to *Nostromo* that he had created a South American country from a single "glimpse" of the continent he had had as a sailor. Sherry proves that Conrad, in fact, read extensively about that region. Imagination moved Conrad's story far beyond remembered sources.[92]

In the literary world William Empson is best known for the boldness of his critical insights into literature. He was also a fine poet. In or about 1970 in Oxford, I was invited by John Wain to join him at a lecture hall to hear Empson speak about "The Rime of the Ancient Mariner." What I didn't know was that Empson was going to bring Coleridge's poem to life with such extraordinary intimacy that one seemed to be standing beside the poet as he must have gazed in 1798 or thereabouts at the Bristol Channel and beheld one of the most horrifying sights in the Western world. Empson himself, whom John and I would meet at a pub after the lecture, was still sprightly running in his declining years, belying the small stature, thin, graying hair, and spectacles. He was warm, humorous, and companionable, and I mention his *élan* because I take on faith what he revealed in his lecture, though I haven't confirmed his thesis elsewhere.

It was this: lines 171 through 186 of the poem, previously regarded as obscure, are at the very heart of its meaning. Here are the crucial lines:

> *When that strange ship drove suddenly*
> *Betwixt us and the Sun.*
>
> *And straight the Sun was flecked with bars . . .*
> *As if through a dungeon grate, he peered*
> *With broad and burning face . . .*
>
> *Are those her ribs through which the Sun*
> *Did peer, as through a grate?*

The Mariner in his own vessel has seen approaching it a ghostly ship with a crew of two, Death and Life-in-Death. When the ships collide, all of the Mariner's shipmates die. At first glance this sequence seems a picturesque description of a calamity brought upon sinners as divine retribution for the killing of an albatross, the sort of incredulous nonsense one might expect from ill-educated sailors. Death is accompanied by Life-in-Death, a symbol, as I interpret it, of lives without souls. So there had to be something about that ship which makes it "strange," makes it akin to a "dungeon," gives it "ribs", as if it were an active skeleton, a ghostly warrant for punishment by God. The bars and ribs are not just silhouetted against a Sun that, "burning," is very much alive. Whatever they represent on Earth, they contaminate and print evil on the solar system, the source of life.

Empson found a "live" source for the imagery, a simple, hideous, and quite specific source near Nether Stowey where Coleridge was living at the time he wrote the poem. Nether Stowey is located near the Bristol Channel. Beached on its shores and within sight of Coleridge's cottage were the rotting remains of ships that had been used for the trafficking of black slaves. The poem, published in *Lyrical Ballads* in 1798, seems to anticipate the abolition of slavery that will actually occur in England a few years later. We feel as if we are peering over Coleridge's shoulder at an abomination and can hear him exclaim with empathy and compassion words of the Mariner that one hundred years later are fully soul-wrenching in words of Conrad's Kurtz from the heart of darkness: "The horror! The horror!"

CHAPTER 8

Destiny

Imagination, usually as elusive as Leviathan, can sometimes be glimpsed just below the surface of a story, gliding along in the form of Destiny or Fate. I prefer the term *destiny*, the term *fate* being tangled up with Greek drama in which it is objectified and with *Macbeth* in which it is personified.

In the study of dramatic and fictional forms of literature we rely upon a critical vocabulary without philosophical resonance. For the interrelationship of the main events in a play or a novel we use the term *plot* as if a story were a burial ground or a cleverly planned conspiracy. To assist us in understanding the structure of a story we use *exposition, complication, climax* and *denouement*. Do these words convey the possibility of a universal order? I don't think so. Do these words help us as students and writers to be aware of the awesome nature of our task? I don't think so. And yet writers are both playing God and bowing down before a mystery.

About the term *conflict*, as it applies to storytelling, since I love action, I have no objection. A story is in many respects a war. Like a war, it is a protracted engagement in which battles are waged and won or lost, and victories, though often dubious, may have moral meaning. Even if we already know the result of a conflict, we still ponder and seek to comprehend those actions—historical, psychological, cultural—that may have been responsible for that result. If characters and events cross over, ever so slightly, into the territory of fantasy or delusion, we suspend disbelief, and sometimes conflict in a literary work is *not* a war. Wars are messy while stories have clear resolutions. Parting company with history and biography, stories, properly executed, have an ineluctable quality. Historians and biographers may quarrel about facts and their meanings, but poets and fiction writers provide an indisputable connection between events and their causes, thereby raising in literature beyond entertainment and escape the consciousness of readers and members of an audience. Resolution is revelation. What is revealed is the nebulous influence of destiny.

A concern with destiny reminds us that there is an order that is both "in" us and "beyond" us. When the spectacle of the world is both "seen" and "unseen," we get a glimpse of purposive laws possibly governing our existence. Destiny in literature, then, means that there may be an *inherent form* in the movement from Being to Becoming. Destiny in literature suggests that some strange power directs the course of events.

It's the fire within, surely.

We recognize destiny in cause-and-effect relationships of all kinds, usually in the interplay of individuals and society but also in cause-and-effect relationships between peoples and the conditions of their time and place, including relationships to the land to which they are or are not attuned.

How do we know that there is inherent form in many a literary work? I've asked Shakespeare to help me out with this question, and he has graciously consented to let me fall on my face.

If inherent form has been disturbed, as it is in *Romeo and Juliet*, we realize that the play is in essence a comedy that turns out tragically. It does not build with inherently tragic materials even though there is lots of bad luck to illustrate our susceptibility to misfortune. There is no reason for the vendetta between Montagues and Capulets. It's an unexplored "given." When Romeo and Juliet have succeeded in outwitting their bloody-minded families, and when they have come within sight of making their escape and starting a new life somewhere else, a letter fails to arrive on time, a plan collapses, and love finds its end in the double suicide in the tomb. "Where the comedies celebrate order by moving from disharmony to harmony," John Wain concludes from his studies of Shakespeare, "this play moves from surface disharmony to an almost-achieved surface harmony, before being dashed by a blow from its author's fist into fundamental, irremediable disaster."[93] The anticipated tragic vision dissolves into pathos. Today, I suppose, the lovers would have cellphones and avoid suicide.

The conversion of luck or incredible coincidence into something foreordained—*planted* in exposition so as to avoid the distasteful "surprise ending"—serves to solve the problem of suitable form. Then destiny can spin plot. This is what happens in *Hamlet*. I don't know whether Shakespeare was a Christian, a believer in a God or Providence that is responsible for damnation or salvation, but Hamlet, the character, is. His devotion enables the play which carries his name to move from Letter A, the *donnée*, the given, the theme, the basic assumption, through the alphabet soup of a rising action of cause-and-effect relationship to Letter Z, the destination. Conflict has not been "jumped." Inherently tragic materials have been built. Moreover, when bad luck turns out to be good luck at a strategically located time offstage between Act IV and Act V, Providence, a power that Hamlet is finally convinced gives justification for his actions, selects him, as it were, as instrument for His, God's vengeance. If we approach the play, therefore, as a Christian play, whatever other kind of play it may be, we bear in mind and try to swallow the Biblical injunction that vengeance is God's business, not man's. When the ghost of the slain king appears to the prince, and Hamlet has satisfied himself that angels and ministers of grace don't need to defend him against this immigrant, he realizes he has been born to set things right. As a Renaissance prince, he's quite ready to leap to revenge as long as it isn't *his* revenge, the fatal mistake made by Laertes later in the play. Hamlet doesn't want to show up at the Last Judgment with some bad karma. Yet that's exactly what will happen after he kills Polonius, and the question is, will he still deserve divine mercy? Ironically, when King Claudius is at prayer, Hamlet seems to rationalize a failure to kill the old boy, for if Hamlet kills a man who is communicating with God, that man goes to Heaven. What kind of revenge is that? Of course, Claudius lets the audience know that his prayers had been futile. Perhaps the irony means tough luck, Hamlet, and there's more to come, but we know before Hamlet knows that *inevitability* is moving along quite nicely. We come to that seemingly ridiculous volte-face offstage. The ship which is carrying Hamlet to death in England is captured by pirates, friendly chaps at that. Rosencrantz and Guildenstern, those treacherous college buddies, are sent to *their* lovely execution. Now at last Hamlet can do something about all that Danish rot because his vengeance is divinely ordained. Hamlet is certain of his destiny, and flights of angels will probably guide him to his rest.

The concept of destiny as making us aware of inherent form in literature helps us, I think, to grasp the connection between literature and life. Sometimes, though, we are going to be disappointed. Why, for instance, is D.H. Lawrence's novel *Lady Chatterley's Lover* so inadequately conceived it resembles soft pornography? Although Mellors's seduction of Constance with f-words is just silly and their roll in the hay is, as intended, tender, these characters have little in common and don't sacrifice themselves to a genuine unity, in real life an ordeal. They remain undeveloped, bricks made of straw. Their "relationship" won't, in my opinion, last more than a few months. That's their real, unexplored destiny. Lawrence, I think, was too busy cocking a snook at the upper classes to create complex characters. In any case he fancies himself as a sexually potent, working-class stud. By contrast, F. Scott Fitzgerald's *The Great Gatsby* transmits to us that nebulous influence of destiny. In spite of Hollywood's infatuation with this novel it is more than an entertainment. The reason is clear: it is not Gatsby's story but Nick Carraway's, who tells it. Nick sees himself from the beginning as someone born to give credit to good instincts and decency. He makes every effort throughout the story to present Gatsby in that light of a saving grace, not, however, perceived by others in the cast, the careless and conventional *nouveaux arrivés*, pseudo-intellectuals, and Jazz Age drunks. Nobody comes to Gatsby's funeral but Nick. So, he alone is able to assert solidarity with Gatsby's "capacity for wonder,"[94] and he can do this, we are told, because he's from the Midwest, not Manhattan, not Long Island. Midwesterners, we are told, understand the persistence, even in a glamorous gangster obsessed with unrequited love, of faith in a fresh "green light" of American dreamers. Fitzgerald's novel actually postulates a poignant historical judgment about our land's destiny. That national destiny would not have been imaginatively formulated had Nick Carraway's point of view not prevailed.

I rather envy writers who know where they're going with a story. Its ending isn't then some vague destination at the end of a road originally lacking in yellow bricks. In truth, I have shared with millions of writers the seemingly unbearable anxiety of having to face blank sheets of paper. Wouldn't it be a less stressful proceeding to fill, in advance of actual composition, note-books detailing plot and dramatis personae, rather than begin a journey with little but intuition for a compass? Yes. But why bother to write a story you already know? I myself prefer a middle way: follow a general sketch of events that leaves room for surprises. The completely foreknown story arrives dead on bestseller lists. A lack of anxiety has simply been exchanged for *Ennui*, the modern Devil,[95] while too great a burden of anxiety can lead not only to a loss of confidence but also to depression and suicide. I knew a promising writer in New York who told me that, after reading Joyce's *Ulysses*, he abandoned the novel he was working on and swore never to finish it or undertake to write another one. "*Ulysses*," he revealed to me in an offhand manner, "says everything that needs to be said and says it better than anyone else could hope to say." I agreed that *Ulysses* is a great novel and told him so, in spite of my reservations about any surplus of virtuosity. "It's not scripture," I added. A year later I heard that my friend had become so sickened by alcoholism that he had had to be rushed to Bellevue in an advanced stage of the DTs. This anecdote is not a plea for aspiring writers to steer clear of *Ulysses*. Although Columbus and Magellan may have seen Chinese maps of the globe before they set sail, they didn't lack for a desire to make discoveries.[96] Theirs, I think, is an attitude for serious writers to emulate.

The amazing thing about destiny in imaginative literature is that discoveries may suddenly be made. The character you thought you knew may take on a life of her own. A character who is to you a stranger pops up and takes command of the story you thought you were controlling. The effect you are seeking has a cause you were not anticipating. In short, the literary vocation can leave to the world something that wasn't there before, something previously uncreated. That's a truly inspiring—and responsible—undertaking!

I'll use as an example Taylor Caldwell's *A Pillar of Iron*, an extraordinarily erudite historical novel about the life of Cicero. What could be more politically compelling and relevant to contemporary empire-building than the story of an honest lawyer, perhaps the only man of probity in all of Rome just before Julius Caesar and fellow conspirators seize control? A fictionalized life of Cicero must nevertheless dramatize that humanity and make his heart, not his oratory, not his losing battle for freedom, the story that allows us to see him, understand him, suffer with him. That is why, I presume, Caldwell quite suddenly interrupts the biography of Cicero's youth and has him encounter Livia Curius. He at sight of her falls deeply in love for the first and last time, ever, as follows in rather turgid prose:

> Marcus slowly approached her. She smiled at him without shyness. She was tall and graceful, almost as tall as himself, and near his age . . . She had an air of assurance and simple dignity. Then he could see her more clearly, and he thought he had never seen a girl so lovely. She was like spring, exquisitely formed and budding. Auburn hair flowed far below her waist, burnished in the setting sun, and rippling like water. It seemed to catch fire around her face, which was luminously pale.[97]

Even if Livia was a historical person, which I doubt, I refuse to believe that *this* Livia, *this* Marcus Tullius Cicero, *this* fateful encounter are to be found in the Vatican Library where Caldwell spent years of research.

The relationship of Nature and of Society to people and things may also conjure up the nebulous influence of destiny. George Stewart's *Storm* reveals the cause-and-effect relationship between a force of Nature and the people or things affected by its destructive passage. Emily Brontë's *Wuthering Heights* also brings Nature to the fore. Its Byronic hero, a wild and passionate personification of violent atmosphere, is Heathcliff, *heath* being akin to *heathen*, a primitive individual. Because society in this novel, unlike society in typical nineteenth-century English novels, seems overwhelmed by Nature, one has the impression that *Wuthering Heights* is not an English novel at all but an American one, perhaps traded to us in America for one of the more soporific novels of Henry James. Americans, as I've noted before, prefer wild unbridled liberty to social cooperation. Americans tend to believe that they are naturally virtuous. Twain's *Huckleberry Finn*, for example, lights out for the Territory in order to avoid anyone who will "sivilize" him. During his residence on Sullivan's Island in South Carolina, Edgar Allan Poe must have experienced hurricanes. They would certainly make the fall of the House of Usher seem quite a commonplace event. Faulkner couldn't resist introducing a flood into *As I Lay Dying*, nor did John Williams resist introducing a blizzard in *Butcher's Crossing*. Captain Ahab believes he has the authority to destroy Nature in the "personage" of Moby-Dick, but he gets his comeuppance from that white whale. Relationship to Nature can introduce a force of destiny.

It is curious, but we do not always acknowledge Society as the determining factor in fiction. I'm using the word in its usual cultural sense but with a claustrophobic twist. Franz Kafka was a master at creating Society as a force so powerful it is not a benign urban environment but an actively ominous assailant. The individual in *The Trial*, whose identity has already been reduced to "K," resembles victims in show trials in totalitarian regimes; his "prosecutor" is not a government but a city. Needing no defense and having none, K confesses and accepts that he will be taken to execution amidst cries of execration. Vasily Grossman's *Life and Fate* hits the nail on the head: literature dramatizes human destiny. In his novel Fate is a dead-end without Becoming. Lest we consider Society as completely closed, we need to remind ourselves that some of the greatest novels of the nineteenth century reveal individuals, especially women, as trapped in and suffocated by an otherwise conventionally "normal" bourgeois civilization. Ruefully, perhaps, major English novelists from Richardson, Fielding, and Austen through Thackery and well into our own times seem to accept as necessity a conformity to the manners and mores of a class-conscious, middle-class society; their readers, after all, came from the prospering English middle class. However, Dickens, George Eliot, George Meredith, and Thomas Hardy, followed by D.H. Lawrence, Virginia Woolf, and Joyce Cary, expose the set-ups of the provincial bourgeoisie. Hardy's *Tess of the d'Urbervilles* and *The Return of the Native* are indictments of Society. Few writers were as concerned as Hardy was with suffering, in particular with the human sense of impotence in the face of a ruthless destiny. The female protagonists of Flaubert's *Madame Bovary* and Tolstoy's *Anna Karenina* commit suicide. Society bears much responsibility for these tragedies.

The working-out of destinies in Tolstoy's greatest novels is of the utmost interest because, one, trusting in the imaginative process, he evidently made his stories up as he went along and, two, he, contrary to his intentions in a judgmental way, allowed a character to emerge as wonderfully true to life, according to his or her own determination. Here is what Henri Troyat, Tolstoy's biographer, has to say about *War and Peace*:

> When he began his book, did Tolstoy know what adventures lay in store for his characters from the first line to the last? Everything inclines us to believe he did not: *their destinies as well as their personalities were decided as he went along.* And yet their behavior corresponds to their personalities at every turn. The wildest schemes seem matter-of-fact as if they were proposed by living beings. That is the miracle of Tolstoy: this gift of life that he transmits to hundreds of creatures, all different, lightly yet unforgettably sketched; soldiers, peasants, generals, great noblemen, young maidens and women of the world. He moves from one to the other, effortlessly changing age, sex and social class. He gives each a particular way of thinking and talking, a physical appearance, a weight in live flesh, a past, even an odor. (*Emphasis added*) [98]

Here is what Troyat says about *Anna Karenina*:

> *As to the progression of the scenes, he believed it was the result of some mysterious process over which the author had no control.* "I had proof of this," he wrote to Strakhov, "with Vronsky's suicide. I had never

clearly felt the necessity of it. I had begun to revise my rough draft and suddenly, by some means that was totally unexpected but ineluctable, Vronsky determined to put a bullet through his head, and it later became clear that that scene was organically indispensable. "Do you know, I often sit down to write some specific thing, and suddenly I find myself on a wider road, *the work begins to spread out in front of me. (Emphasis added)*[99]

[Contrary to Tolstoy's intentions] it is the damned who arouse our sympathy and the virtuous who disappoint us. Saddled with every curse that could be laid upon her, Anna Karenina towers so far above all the other characters that the *author was forced* to give the book her name. (*Emphasis added*)[100]

Finally, as Troyat observes, destiny in works of imaginative literature, as the overall result of behavior in fiction and drama, may open out to a grand interpretation of human history. Here's Troyat on both *Anna Karenina* and *War and Peace*:

One strange thing: in both *Anna Karenina* and *War and Peace*, it is the exceptional, glittering beings, those marked by some metaphysical sign, who disappear, and the average, even insignificant ones who survive and trudge along their little paths, halfway between good and evil. . . Anna Karenina and Vronsky are swept from the scene, leaving behind them the mighty conquerors in the battle of life: Kitty and Levin, fine, upstanding, dull young folk, held up as an example by all their neighbors. Is this Tolstoy's plea for mediocrity? No; he simply feels that mankind needs, now and then, these extraordinary beings to shake up the dozing masses; but in the final analysis, it is *the conjunction of innumerable ordinary destinies that carries history forward*. Whether we like it or not, the future belongs to the Rostovs and Bezukhovs and Levins, to the shuffling mob of men of goodwill. (*Emphasis added, titles excepted*) [101]

Speaking for myself, I begin a novel with an idea and an image. If, however, I didn't harbor a mysterious confidence that that image will beget image, my *donnée* would never get off the typewriter. Gradually the interplay of characters with other characters and within themselves begins to assume a life of its own. I introduce method into madness. I establish rules. I will work for four hours or write a thousand words a day, whichever comes first. Before I quit for the day and do the chores, I make sure I know the next sentence. In the interim between one day and the next, I let the story rest in the subconscious. The point to emphasize is that I *seem* to know where I'm going with the story. The reason must be, form *is* inherent, but *proof* that form is inherent will not be revealed until the job is finished! Necessities may be slow to clarify themselves, but, with luck, tempestuous propulsions occur, and unexpected reckonings may prove fair.

I seldom go back to a story after it has been revised for publication. Recently out of curiosity I studied my novels in order to see them as having had, all along, an underlying interpretation of history. Finding sources for them was no trouble at all. When I made diagrams of cause-and-effect relationships, I was astonished to see how these really did reveal the presence of imagination at work: destiny.

Suddenly a Mortal Splendor emerged primarily from memories of places I have visited or actually lived in such as Colorado Springs, London, New Mexico, the Grand Canyon and Santiago de Chile. Chile, I visited in the summer of 1978 when the military government of General Pinochet was at the height of its power. The story of "the disappeared", as revealed by the Archbishop of Chile's Solidarity publications, left a powerful impression. Scenes in Budapest are imaginary but to some degree based upon extensive reading of works translated from the Hungarian. The original image out of which the novel would eventually evolve is that of a little boy who is kicking a soccer ball out in the snow on Christmas Day, 1956, at the Traiskirchen camp for Hungarian refugees. Teaching in London in October of that year when the revolt against the Soviet Empire occurred, I made plans to spend Christmas in Vienna, there to volunteer my services with the International Red Cross. As soon as I was free, I packed a small kit, dressed warmly, grabbed my Olympia typewriter, and bought a third-class rail ticket, arriving in Vienna on Christmas Eve in the midst of a snowstorm. Loudspeakers blatted out "*Stille Nacht*" while I trudged through the streets looking for a hotel that hadn't been shot up by retreating Russians. I found a hotel room, price three dollars, communication in fractured French. Christmas day, I took a trolley car to the camp at Traiskirchen near the Hungarian border. What happened at Traiskirchen and for several days in Vienna I later wrote down at a hostel in Innsbruck on my way back to London. The piece would be published in a Durham newspaper a few weeks later, as follows:

Innsbruck, Austria. Winter arrived early in Vienna. The cypress trees stood clipped and swollen in the parks, and far-off birch flanked hills marched down the sky. On Christmas morning it snowed. Across the boulevard from the dark Imperial Palace some Hungarian boys huddled near a small fire. When the police came the boys stamped out the fire and jumped on a tramcar wheezing and shimmying toward the Opera.

Hungarian refugees are everywhere. They live in the hotels and wait to go to America. They are always waiting. In the cold outside the Kino they wait to see James Dean's last picture or the luxury of a celluloid Las Vegas. If money remained after the Communist official took his bribe, then they wait to see the striptease at the Lido or the Moulin Rouge. If money is wanting, they linger all day in espresso bars or, simply, lounge in the hotels listening to lusty German voices over the radio.

The Rakos family is waiting in a cheap hotel in Praterstern in the former Soviet sector. Everywhere in the Soviet sector a sense of futility clings to bullet-pocked buildings and auto-empty streets. The Rakos family have been here for six weeks.

"So. You are American. Is right?" asks Mrs. Rakos in French.

"Yes."

"It true, then, you have automobile in America?"

"It is true."

"You are a very rich man."

"No, I am not rich."

"Ah," Mrs. Rakos sighs, "how much longer we attend going to America?"

Rakos himself was a weaver in Budapest. He is anxious to work. He did not fight the Communists. One day his brother came to say he should flee, so Rakos, his wife and ten-year-old daughter followed his brother that night through the frozen swamps at the border.

Mrs. Rakos once heard "The Star-Spangled Banner" over Radio Free Europe. She begs you to sing it. After you sing it, everyone shakes hands. Next morning the police come to the hotel to talk to Rakos. There is no word yet from the American Consulate.

Most of the refugees are poor and do not live in Vienna. They live in the sixty camps scattered throughout Austria. The poor ones are waiting too.

Traiskirchen, about thirty miles from Vienna, shelters 4,000 Hungarians in an old army barracks formerly used by the Russians. The bunks, tables, benches and glass windows were taken by the Russians. Heat is supplied by a variety of rusty, potbellied stoves. Sometimes as many as forty men, women and children sleep together in rooms suitable for ten people. During daylight hours many refugees sleep or stare at the ceiling. In the mess hundreds more loaf long after the noonday meal of chocolate and goulash. The young people crowd into a reading room to peruse old torn newspapers or listen to the single radio. *Usually a few men and boys can be found playing football in the courtyard with the camp's sports equipment: a half dozen rubber balls.*

Stefan is thirty years old and was once an architecture student. His face is gaunt and leather-skinned. He spent six years in Communist prison for conspiracy. He learned to speak English in prison. When the revolt came, he decided to take his three-months-old child to freedom. The night he escaped he walked fifty kilometers with the child in his arms. At the border Soviet troops filled the darkness with hissing magnesium flares. Each time a flare exploded Stefan fell to earth clutching his child. Now he hesitates to go to Australia. If he doesn't like Australia, may he later go to America? Perhaps, he thinks, he may wait for the volcano in Hungary to erupt again. He would return to fight.

An American girl with teaching experience in New York slum areas has started a school for the hundreds of children at Traiskirchen. "How can you have a school," she despairs, "without books, pencils, crayons, paper or toys?" The children cluster about her knees quietly—too quietly.

Josef is an old man. Before the Nazis came, he bred racehorses on his own lands. Years of imprisonment under the Nazis and Russians have wasted his tall manly body, and from his scarred, gaptoothed face only the blue eyes shine still with the fierceness of youth. Released from prison a broken man, he was put to work grooming twenty plough horses at a collective farm. Every day the well water they needed he drew up with cramped, freezing hands.

Like many old men Josef talks, but he does not talk of the days of his youth. He talks of Hungary, and as he does so his eyes flash. He talks of Hunyady who stopped the Turks at Nandorfchevvar in the fifteenth century, of Kossuth who led the revolt against the Empire, of all the violent heroes who have made Hungarians proud.

"But why?" he pleads with his bent body. "Why did America not come when we needed her?"

What is the use explaining the dilemma to Josef?

"We showed you that the Soviet will go when you force him. Ah, always it is Hungary who must sacrifice her body before the invader so that the West may prosper in science and the arts."

"The world will not let you down."

Josef shakes his head. "You are American and young. But I am glad I meet you. You have made me calm."

In time you leave Vienna, Traiskirchen and the refugees far behind. Winter, early and cruel for them, seems paradise to you in the Tyrol. Little villages snuggle in the valleys between incredible peaks, and the bulbous cupolas of the Tyrolean churches lance the air like brass Victorian bedposts. Skiers criss-cross on the slopes and soar birdlike into the air. But you do not forget the Rakos family, Stefan and the American schoolteacher. Most of all you do not forget Josef, who still waved his hand from the platform as your train stole into the night. (*Emphasis added*)

Almost forty years later the little boy who had been in the group which was playing soccer appeared to me in a vision and said, *Tell my story*.

In *Suddenly a Mortal Splendor*, I named the boy Paul and told his story.

Paul is first-person narrator and protagonist whose story takes him from Budapest to a refugee camp near Vienna, to a home in London, to the United States and foreign countries as a soldier, and to Chile, which he, himself, fictionalizes as "Pacífica" out of fear of repercussions from secret agencies. A terrifying dystopia, one where freedoms are curtailed and widespread economic deprivation is experienced, is primarily anchored by historical events: my 29 October 1951 experience of an atomic test; the 22 October 1956 Hungarian revolution against Soviet domination since the end of the Second World War in 1945; the U.S.-sponsored military coup d'état against the elected Chilean government in October 1973, with General Pinochet installed as president and employing "disappearance" of political dissidents and others; the Act of Congress, also in the 'seventies, whereby Navajo Indians in Arizona are forcibly relocated from ancestral lands (by any definition an act of genocide). A fifth historical event, one which occurred in 1979 at Church Rock, New Mexico, went virtually unreported in *The New York Times* even though it represented, I believe, the largest radioactive spill of nuclear waste in history up to that time. Contamination reached the Little Colorado River in Arizona and was carried from there to Hoover Dam, thence to California. Actions in *Splendor* are locked in to these events. The point I wish to make is that a strange story blossomed out of a simple *donnée* and ended with an entirely unforeseen novel about human destiny.

It remains a mystery to me how the image of a little Hungarian boy's kicking a ball during a snowstorm in an overcrowded refugee camp could have produced an avalanche of other images until that boy, grown into a veteran Army sergeant in the Vietnam War, would find in the egotistical and morally odious character of John Woolpack not only a father-figure he could love but also a visionary for whom human destiny was interlocked with the fate of the Earth. Father-son relationships, in literature as in life, form a universal story, often tentative and painfully shy. Moreover, one of the secrets of characterization in fiction and drama is to make seemingly ill-suited, disreputable, and tyrannous men and women into lovers. Margaret Mitchell, seldom recognized as the master of irony she was, grasped this secret of a storyteller's nettle. Scarlett O'Hara and Rhett Butler in *Gone with the Wind* are, on the one hand, contemptible, on the other hand, totally unforgettable characters whom millions of readers love. To a degree, perhaps, I foresaw in the evolution of a plot that Paul would find relief when Woolpack commits suicide in order to gain the release of his daughter from captivity. What I didn't anticipate, however, was that Woolpack's self-sacrifice was predestined not by my conscious contrivance but by an imaginative leap. When Woolpack deliberately falls into the toxic waters of radioactive waste, he does so, as I almost unwittingly described it, in the "attitude of a crucifixion." And so, he must have been destined, all along, *as a person with a new consciousness*. His "mortal splendor," coming "suddenly"—the novel's title comes from a poem by Robinson Jeffers—is adventitious, coming from the fire within.

The imagined revelation of a fictional character focused for me my own long-felt but inadequately centered concern for the fate of the Earth. For years I took the planet for granted. Although I witnessed an atomic test in Nevada, I remembered the atomic blast as a beautiful event rather than as a portent of earthly catastrophe. Similarly, today, my awareness of the disappearance of planetary life is just beginning to be increased.

With discovery of theme I found where I had been going from the beginning as a writer, in a sense my own destiny. The result is a quartet of novels that constitute a single work on the century before, during, and after the Atomic Age. *The Door of the Sad People* opens the Century with the story of a Colorado youth's spiritual growth from abused childhood into an artist during a struggle for human rights as immigrant miners—like those in Colorado's Ludlow Massacre in 1914—encounter forces gathering inexorably toward total war. *The Voice of the Children in the Apple Tree* surveys the continent from North and South to West and from the civilization of old-fashioned American conscience and rectitude to the new world of the Atomic Age in 1945, then envisions in the lives of steadfast lovers a future recovery of innocence. *The Cold War of Kitty Pentecost*, set in the South in the 1960s, continues the Century in the tradition of Shakespeare's Romeo and Juliet—star-crossed lovers doomed by separation during World War II, by dread of nuclear annihilation, and by generations of racism. *Suddenly a Mortal Splendor* closes the Century and completes the quartet with an overview of the fate of the Earth as compassion and sacrifice prevail over global violence, the final scene at the Grand Canyon representing a coming world of consciousness and the eternal and sacred beauty of nature.

CHAPTER 9

Imagination as a Force for Peace and Survival

No man is an island, entire of itself; every man is a piece of the continent, a part of the main. . . Any man's death diminishes me because I am involved in mankind.
—John Donne, *Meditation XVII*

Imagination is a force of consciousness, one of the ways we think. It has the power to control, influence, or produce an effect. The *literary* imagination, in particular, exemplifies this force or power in a variety of ways but especially through metaphor. Where comparison, simile, and analogy casually make "A" *like* "B," metaphor insists that "A" **is** "B," thereby uniting or fusing them into "C," a transferring more searching and profound than that in the other figures of speech. If we view a metaphor's potentiality in the context of our involvement with mankind, as Donne does, we become increasingly aware of how individual ("island") actions fuse into something more organized ("continent"), eliciting an in-the-same-boat spirit. Imagination as a force of consciousness can change anything except nature itself.

There is a great deal of literature about war. Not only does literature poach upon such related disciplines as philosophy, political science, psychology, and sociology, it also proceeds along lines of inquiry associated with the mathematical and physical sciences. Furthermore, because literary study necessarily involves investigation of verbal signs and symbols, some of us find ourselves pondering the meaning of myths, because mythologies are imaginative creators of all religions, all cultures. In other words, imagination has very much to do with war and peace. It has even been said that all wars are holy wars. Whether true or not, the statement suggests the complicity between aggression and culture and opens the possibility, from a humanistic perspective at least, of understanding the problem of human survival--a very real problem indeed.

Mythology has been seriously studied only in recent years. We mark its progress from the publication in 1890 of Sir James Frazer's *The Golden Bough: A Study in Magic and Religion*, through the depth psychology of Freud and especially of Jung whose theory of a Collective Unconscious burst the crust of rationalistic dogma, and to, in our own time, the monumental works on mythology of Joseph Campbell. My indebtedness to Campbell will be apparent to anyone familiar with such books as *The Hero With a Thousand Faces* (1949), *The Masks of God* (in four volumes, 1959-1968), and *Myths to Live By* (1972).[102] The latter book contains a chapter entitled "Mythologies of War and Peace," and from this I shall borrow extensively, even without paraphrase, occasionally elaborating upon its insights. We need a professional and visionary "anthropologist" to give a grandstand view of the subject in order to evaluate calmly our present condition in the Atomic Age.

Campbell discerns as the basic idea of practically every war mythology that the enemy is a monster and that in killing him one is protecting the only truly valuable order of human life on earth, which is that, of course, of one's own people. The Orient and tropical zones aside, the two most important war mythologies in the West have been Homer's *Iliad* and the Old Testament. Let us, closely following Campbell, examine these stories as myths, calling the Greek epic an example of the myth of heroic war and the Hebrew epic an example of the myth of holy war.

Though steeped in gore, the *Iliad* is irradiated by moments of humanity. In Book VI the Trojan hero Hector, soon to be slain in battle by the Greek hero Achilles, bids farewell to Andromache, his wife, and their little son Astyanax. Their fate is all but certain: Hector, slain, will have his corpse dishonored by Achilles, and Andromache and Astyanax will be put to the sword or enslaved. Hector, we are told, smiled in silence as he looked on his son, but Andromache, letting her tears fall, spoke to him:

> Dearest, your own great strength will be your death, and you have
> no pity on your little son, nor on me, ill-starred, who soon must be
> your widow; for presently the Achaeans, gathering together, will set

> upon you and kill you; and for me it would be far better to sink into
> the earth when I have lost you, for there is no other consolation for
> me after you have gone to your destiny--only grief.

And Hector answered:

> Poor Andromache! Why does your heart sorrow so much for me?
> No man is going to hurl me to Hades, unless it is fated, but as for
> fate, I think that no man yet has escaped it once it has taken its first
> form, neither brave man nor coward.

Little Astyanax, we are told, shrank in fear from his father's gleaming helmet, but Hector removed it, kissed his son and prayed for him to Zeus before departing. Although Hector is fighting for his family as much as for Troy, he expects everyone he holds dearest to remain unflinchingly faithful in all circumstances and to share with him that heroic spirit fretting at the limitations set on human effort and striving to break through them by some prodigious exertion and achievement. In refusing to surrender his manliness and decency, Hector appears as morally superior to the Greeks.

Campbell makes the point about Homer's humanity, that it shows with what respect and great capacity for empathy the ancient Greeks could regard their enemies. Moreover, they could regard the heroic spirit, when put to the test of war, as of dubious value. The motive for the sack of Troy is vengeance: Helen deserted her dull husband for a Trojan prince, so some of the Greek gods, we are told, favored war to get her back, though other gods supported Troy. When we move from the *Iliad* to the *Odyssey*, the myth of heroic war collides with a narrative about values of home and peace. Heroes like Achilles, dead for twenty years, report from Hades that perhaps life would have been better, after all, in a quiet cottage in the countryside. Agamemnon, co-leader of the Greeks at Troy, has been murdered by a faithless wife; his brother Menelaos, though alive in Lacedaemon, has *his* faithless wife home again, but Helen is a sulky vixen who expresses little remorse for the past. Odysseus himself, whose intelligence has frustrated his own ends, has become a bit of a veteran bore who weeps to hear his own exploits recounted and really has nothing to do save flex his aging muscles and dream of slaughtering his wife's suitors, over a hundred of them. Even Odysseus's dog dies on a dung heap at sight of him as if to reproach the master for having left home to fight a war "for a whore" (as Daniel Defoe summarizes the affair).

The Greek playwrights Aeschylus (525-456 B.C.) and Sophocles (497-406 B.C.) continue the tradition of depicting enemies as human. Aeschylus himself fought the invading Persians at Salamis yet humanized them in his tragedy, *The Persians*. In *Agamemnon* his uncompromising conception of human responsibility comes close to a virtual condemnation of war as a cultural aberration: the goddess Artemis, protectress of the innocent and unborn, will not allow Zeus, an Olympian tyrant, to get away with the sacrifice of Agamemnon's daughter (a pretext for war) or with the destruction of Troy, and, when Queen Clytemnestra, having murdered her husband, announces that war crimes are expiated and utopian peace has arrived, it is clear from the play's tragic irony that historical justice has not been accomplished. Sophocles, like Aeschylus, also explores the ambiguities of violence but emphasizes a sacred view of life which may preserve mankind and the earth we inhabit. For example, *Antigone* begins after a fratricidal war in which one of the heroine's brothers has been slain, his body thrown out to rot and be eaten by wild dogs. The tyrant Creon then forbids anyone on pain of death from offering burial rites to the fallen enemy. Antigone defies his authority, buries her brother, and is entombed and driven to suicide. So, one of the themes of the play is that rituals are needed to prevent the increase of the killing mania. Burial of a warrior, notably an enemy of state, carries the life principle back to Mother Earth for rebirth.

However, it would be a mistake to believe that the Greeks, in general, ever thought it desirable or even possible to love their enemies. Greek civilization centered itself in legends about heroic wars of the late Bronze and early Iron Age masters of the Aegean. Consider the marble friezes taken from the Parthenon by Lord Elgin and now displayed in the British Museum: they depict a mythical battle between Lapiths, whose figures are human, and Centaurs, whose bodies are half human, half animal. In other words, the conflict of civilization and barbarism is in the nature of necessity, and the banner of civilization is necessarily Greek. It is *our* fully human people overcoming *those* less-than-human, more or less monstrous people. Meanwhile on Mount Olympus, divinities quarrel among themselves while directing human quarrels below. A polytheistic pantheon of gods could thus favor both sides of a war simultaneously. Therefore the "barbarians" like Trojans and Persians could sometimes be comprehended in their humanity. Most of the time, the myth of heroic war merely perpetuates the idea of the superior order of one's own tribe.

Among the Greeks' approximately contemporaneous neighbors in the ancient Near East were some tribes overrunning Canaan, one of them the earliest Hebrews. Their god is singular, Yahweh, and His sympathies are forever on one side. Accordingly, the enemy depicted in the Old Testament is not even half-human. He's subhuman, a monster to be wasted by Yahweh's chosen people. We are now violently to be indoctrinated in the mythological ambiance of holy war.

Just how holy, one may judge from some typically brutal passages from the Mosaic or Deuteronomic traditions:

> When the Lord your God brings you into the land which you are entering to occupy and drives out many nations before you--Hittites, Giggashites, Amorites, Canaanites, Perizzites, Hivites, and Jebusites, seven nations more numerous and powerful than you--when the Lord your God delivers them into your power and you defeat them, you must put them to death. You must not make a treaty with them or spare them. You must not intermarry with them, neither giving your daughters to their sons nor taking their daughters for your sons; if you do, they will draw your sons away from the Lord and make them worship other gods. Then the Lord will be angry with you and will quickly destroy you. But this is what you must do to them: pull down their altars, break their sacred pillars, hack down their sacred poles and destroy their idols by fire, for you are a people holy to the Lord your God; the Lord your God chose you out of all nations on earth to be his special possession. (Deut. 7:1-6)

> When you advance on a city to attack it, make an offer of peace. If the city accepts the offer and opens its gates to you, then all the people in it shall be put to forced labor and shall serve you. If it does not make peace with you but offers battle, you shall besiege it, and the Lord your God will deliver it into your hands. You shall put all its males to the sword, but you may take the women, the dependents, and the cattle for yourselves, and plunder everything else in the city. You may enjoy the use of the spoil of your enemies which the Lord your God gives you. That is what you shall do to cities at a great distance, as opposed to those which belong to nations near at hand. In the cities of these nations whose land the Lord your God is giving you as a patrimony, you shall not leave any creature alive. You shall annihilate them--Hittites, Amorites, Canaanites, Perizzites, Hivites, Jebusites--as the Lord your God commanded you, so that they may not teach you to imitate all the abominable things that they have

done for their gods and so cause you to sin against the Lord your God. (Deut. 20:10-18)

Is this the same Yahweh who commanded, "Thou shalt not kill"? The myth of holy war continues in the Book of Joshua. After the trumpets and the fall of Jericho, as we read: "they destroyed everything in the city; they put everyone to the sword, men and women, young and old, and also cattle, sheep, and asses." (Joshua 6:21). On and on the holy massacres are accomplished in the name of the local deity until Jerusalem, itself, is besieged and taken by the King of Babylon, Nebuchadnezzar, in the year 586 B.C. (II Kings 25), beginning the so-called period of exile.

Campbell notes that the Old Testament may beguile us with a vision of peace such as that in Isaiah 65:22-25 which echoes that of Isaiah 11:6-9 (the so-called First Isaiah who lived before the exilic period):

> My people shall live the long life of a tree,
> and my chosen shall enjoy the fruit of their labour.
> They shall not toil in vain or raise children for misfortune.
> For they are the offspring of the blessed of the Lord
> and their issue after them;
> before they call to me, I will answer,
> and while they are still speaking, I will listen.
> The wolf and the lamb shall feed together
> and the lion shall eat straw like cattle.
> They shall not hurt or destroy in all my holy mountain says the Lord.

This beautiful passage from the post-exilic Third Isaiah is unfortunately preceded by the usual call for a bloodbath: "The nation or kingdom which refuses to serve you shall perish, and wide regions shall be laid utterly waste" (Isaiah 60:12).

The Old Testament is not our only literature about divinely authorized war. Muslims have the *Koran* that reveals Mohammed as the ultimate prophet. From him, since the seventh century A.D., has been derived a mythology of unrelenting war in God's name, the *jihad* or Holy War. According to this concept, it is the duty of every Moslem male who is free, of full age, in full possession of his intellectual powers, and physically fit for service to fight in the cause of Truth and to conquer all lands not belonging to the territory of Islam.

The international terrorism today, often a perversion of Islam, has deep roots.

Our Western world has its own version of the myth of holy war--the crusade ("bearing of the cross"). The message conveyed by Christendom has often been governed by sentiments of hatred, with love reserved for the elected communicants. At the height of the Middle Ages, under Pope Innocent III (1198-1216), the Church authorized the genocide of a million people in the south of France, yet the victims of this Albigensian Crusade had, like Jesus, explicitly rejected the sword for lives of ascetic purity in peace. The crusading mania accounts for the slaughter of, among other peoples, the native inhabitants of Hispanic America and of North America where Christianized Euro-Americans have sought for centuries to stamp out "heathen"--and peaceful--Indian beliefs and ceremonies.

The myth of heroic war and the myth of holy war have in common a belief in divine authorization for the dehumanizing of the enemy and for the glorifying of invaders and the home folks. Closely related to these myths is the myth of terminal war--the Apocalypse. The basic idea is that there will be a series of wars followed by the end of historic time and the subsequent restoration of the right people to a universal reign of peace under a King of Kings. We encounter here the idea of the Messiah, first envisioned by the pre-exilic prophets as simply an ideal king on David's throne but then in the post-exilic period as a King of Kings who, at the end of time, should be given everlasting dominion over all peoples. Where did this post-exilic idea come from? Not, according to Campbell, from the Hebrews but from the Persians, for whom the first King of Kings was Cyrus the Great. When Babylon fell to him in 539 B.C., he restored peoples to their homelands and governed them through subordinate kings of their own races and traditions. It is Cyrus who is celebrated in Isaiah 45 as a virtual Messiah--but now the servant of Yahweh doing Yahweh's work so that it would ultimately not be the Persians but the people of Yahweh who would reign over the world. As we know, the myth of terminal war, allied with the idea of a Messiah who will resurrect the dead and rule the guiltless, has been in vogue among Christians for two thousand years. The anticipated savior, of course, is Christ, even though the original savior was Persian.

The names for the combatants in terminal war were also adopted from Persian mythology, specifically from Zoroaster or Zarathustra, a Persian prophet of the sixth century B.C.: the powers of Light would achieve victory over the powers of Darkness after a season of general wars and the arrival of an ultimate savior whose name was Saoshyant. Surely it is no coincidence that the

Dead Sea Scrolls of the last century B.C. predict a terminal war to be fought between "the Sons of Light" and "the Sons of Darkness." The Essenes seem to have been a community preparing itself for an imminent Apocalyse that they were elected to survive for all eternity. Whether John the Baptist and Jesus were members of the Essene sect or influenced by it, we may only speculate, but it is clear that Jesus delivered his own version of the apocalyptic message and that Christianity came to birth in an atmosphere of widespread despair (caused by the Roman occupation of Palestine) and of panic (caused by belief in the end of the world). Christian eschatology (i.e., concern with ultimate things such as a Day of Judgment) has continued to make a powerful appeal for two thousand years. For example--and the spectacle is indeed touching-- there are good people right now preparing to sit on deck-chairs on a rooftop in Brooklyn Heights, there to witness the destruction of New York City, one of the places evidently designated for the wrath of God. In banalized form this eschatological concern with war between light and dark forces can be discov- ered in a movie like *Star Wars* and its sequels. The point here is that all end- of-the-world thinking is based on the apocalyptic premise of terminal war, its survivors an elect people. The exception to this rule is nuclear annihilation in which there would be no survivors. More about that presently.

Although the teachings of Jesus have their apocalyptic drift, they rep- resent our best-known mythology of peace. Now the sentiment of love is to prevail according to laws of God. Instead of affirming that life is war, we are to renounce war as well as other concerns of the flesh. Consider Matthew 10:34-36: "You must not think that I have come to bring peace to the earth; I have not come to bring peace, but a sword." What Jesus meant by reference to a sword seems to be clarified in Matthew 26:50-52 in the scene of his ar- rest in the Garden of Gethsemane: "They then came forward, seized Jesus, and held him fast. At that moment one of those with Jesus reached for his sword and drew it, and he struck at the High Priest's servant and cut off his ear. But Jesus said to him, 'Put up your sword. All who take the sword die by the sword.'" Clearly, a very special if not impossible discipline is being called for: absolute abandonment of all the concerns of normal secular life such as family ties and community *and* a renunciation of violence. I, speaking only for myself and not attributing the opinion to Campbell (though I believe he shared it), consider ascetic renunciation of the world as a *negative* aspect of the mythology of peace. Its negativeness need not be construed as a criticism of Christian sacrifice or of the achievements, via nonviolence, of a Gandhi or a Martin Luther King. But we sometimes overlook the marvelously *positive* aspect of Jesus's peace teaching--it is the teaching that cost him his life--and that is *atonement*. Here the emphasis shifts from penal atonement for sins to an atonement, a universal turn-the-cheek confraternity based upon the simple, radical, world-transforming theological doctrine that God the Father has come down, so to say, is joined with the Son and through the Son is conjoint with all humanity. Jesus transforms myths of war and the apocalyptic theme from a historical future to, as Campbell perceives, a psychological present. The battle of good and evil has, as it were, already been resolved, and we are to love our enemies because the Kingdom of God is here and now, though we see it not.

We must ask, again presently, whether this positive atonement is merely a wish-fulfilling ideal or a moral and psychological emergence of increased awareness irrespective of its originally theological, hence mythic conception. If the individual is the source of wonder and is naturally equipped with the power to be "at one" with mankind, we have a gospel, if not a guarantee, of survival.

The ancient myths of war that we have surveyed largely from Joseph Campbell's work, and that I have classified as myths of heroic, holy, and terminal war, are very much alive in today's world. Even heroic war, though seemingly a dinosaur, has been usurped for revolutionary purposes as "the people's heroic struggle" and all that. But at least since the seventeenth century in the modern West there has evolved a realization that it is men, not divinities, who authorize war and wage it. Men also authorize peace and make it. We live, in part, in a *demythologized* world because imaginative writers have conceived of better governments.

There is at least one modern myth of war, that of the just war, which is mythical precisely because it elevates to absolute status the relative abstractions of thought, such as "rights," "humanity," "reason," "history" and "nature," all spelled with initial capital letters and all variously appealed to as if they embodied universal ethical laws. An early example is Hugo Grotius's treatise, *The Rights of War and Peace*, published in 1625 during the Thirty Years War that was devastating Europe. Beginning with the idea that there is a kinship among humanity established by nature, Grotius sees in this bond a community of rights. The society of nations, including as it does the whole human race, needs recognition of these rights, nor do the accidents of geographic boundary obliterate a human demand for justice that springs from the nature of man as a moral being. There is, therefore, his argument goes, a Natural Law that, when properly apprehended, is perceived to be the expression and dictate of Right Reason. Moreover, this Law of Nations is also based upon a system of consent, of practically recognized rules of procedure. In sum, war and peace issues involve ethical principles and can be enforced by rational, mutual interest. One can wage a just war because it is the expression of sovereignty.

The myth of just war lives today deeply in our thinking and remembrance. To name a few "just" wars, we have the American Revolution, the American Civil War, and the Second World War (in its anti-totalitarian, anti-racist aspect). So-called "wars of liberation" are usually considered justifiable, although those who have suffered liberation Communist-style, which is to say totalitarian, discover that the revolution has yet to be decided in terms of justice and freedom. Still, Communists have justified aggression on the basis of capital-H History just as fascists have justified theirs on the basis of capital-N Nature. Like other myths of war, the myth of just war assumes that *our* tribe, nation, or people are enlightened and the *other* people, their leaders at least, are monsters.[103]

War mythologies ancient and modern affirm war as life and life as war. Our roles in the social realm are those of murder's perpetrators or of its victims. Either way, we are accustomed to believe in a future when blood-guilt can be expiated, the pious elected and redeemed, the biological and cultural heritage transmitted to future generations. True, we think, war is a disaster--but no more than the sum of fallen cities, killed and injured people, mourning survivors. Which is to say the sum is never the total of living things converted to corpses. Even when totalitarianism attempts to erase the factual record of past and present, counter forces based in imagination's embrace of Oneness have hitherto existed to preserve the record in human remembrance lest we forget the death-camps and Gulags, the "disappearances" and genocides. It seems possible to go on holding life as sacred and invoking divinities and moral absolutes of somebody's tribe, somewhere (we always think it is ours).

Suddenly since 1945 we can imagine--we *must* imagine--a world in which no one survives nuclear war and all life has been foreclosed where any future is concerned. In that event, life is not only not sacred but worthless. Moreover, the extinction of the species cannot, save by a perversion of religion, be attributed to God's will when it is we ourselves who possess the means to unleash the utterly meaningless, completely unjustified weapons of annihilation. This would not be a Day of Judgment in which God destroys the world but raises the dead and metes out perfect justice to everyone who has ever lived. The complete destruction of mankind by men is an apocalyptic premise without apocalyptic promise.

Surprisingly, the author of *The Fate of the Earth* (1982), Jonathan Schell, was attacked as arrogant and pretentious for his eloquent and grimly passionate description of the apocalyptic premise. Yet it is scientifically accurate, and the fact that it has not been scientifically validated by nuclear holocaust--exactly Schell's point--does not amount to pretense. We do indeed have weapons of such character and magnitude that they could annihilate the species and contaminate the earth. Scientific knowledge, Schell writes, has brought us face to face with "the death of mankind" and in doing so has "caused a basic change in the circumstances in which life was given to us, which is to say that we have altered the human condition."[104] The fact is, for the first time in history we live in a *post*-war posture, or we don't live at all. Our only probable peace arrives *this* side of *one* nuclear war and makes of the whole earth a new historical dimension founded upon ethical and ecological principles.

Although our choice is probably between peace and total annihilation, the most terrible reality mankind has ever faced may still be graced with enough time for us to deal with it. Schell wants instant relief from peril, meaning abolition of nuclear arms, abolition of sovereignty, and abolition, somehow, of aggressive instinct. I hope he has oversimplified the nature of the dangers we face. Although they are frightening, unreasoning fear of them can lead to unwise and destructive behavior. Do nuclear weapons make nuclear war inevitable? Does nuclear war mean the end of the human race? Even to allow logical probability to these questions does not mean that nuclear weapons will be abolished all at once, sovereignty surrendered all at once to a nebulous world order, and violence extirpated from human nature.

Few, I think, still believe the earth is flat. Or that the earth is the center of the cosmos instead of a blip on the tail of one galaxy among billions of galaxies. Or believe that a mountain called Purgatory rises in the South Atlantic toward a heavenly mansion presided over by a gender-coded anthropomorphic deity originally seated there by Babylonian priest-mathematicians. Yet not so long ago, historically considered, these mythic images constituted a cosmology for various clergies, and woe to the seers and stargazers who experienced something else and said so! Put simply: mythologies, as they lose support through imaginings, undergo change and may do so again under pressure of a technological reality of nuclear-arms potential. Our heritage of war myths can be discarded and the authorities behind the myths unmasked until we see the warmakers for what they always were: ourselves. We have never abolished war before, so let's make a start by abolishing the myths of war.

Demythologizing has already, I assume, been in progress for untold centuries. The myth of heroic war, encouraging the valorous to assert their vitality and individuality and to earn values from struggle, itself, belongs by definition to heroic culture, an anachronism like Don Quixote. The myth of holy war finds little support even though jihadists terrorize nations; and in the nuclear age there is no local, tribal aim or ideal worthy of any people whatsoever. Now we peer down from the moon and see our global village as she is, a small, lonely speck of dust lost amidst infinities of dark space. The only truly valuable order of life on earth is that of all people everywhere. And the myth of terminal war should surely be relegated to the nursery. There is no human basis, let alone a scientific one, for postulating an end-of-the-world kingdom of peace to be ruled for all eternity by a savior, unless one is not mortified to imagine a few survivors of the nuclear holocaust. Although men of good will serve us well by spreading gospel, we would be better off if we devoted our energies and thoughts to the postponement of terminal war rather than to its certainty. Apocalyptic pronouncements panic us from thought of authentic survival, the high goal for all mankind that requires consideration of the best ideas that lead to the best ways.

The modern myth of just war is a problematic one. That war and peace are issues to be decided by an international law based upon ethical principles and enforced by rational self-interest is an enlightened concept. It is, in fact, the one we try to live by in what is clearly not the best of all possible worlds. The problematic aspect is precisely the mythical: divine authority has dwindled to philosophical abstractions and these, in turn, have become absolute authority for the totalitarian state. The Kingdom of God, which in Jesus's teachings is a here-and-now spiritual (we might say psychological) reality, has become a monolithic secular kingdom that promises peace, but "peace" without justice or freedom, the "peace" of the police-state. For peoples in historically despotic regions the idea of total state authority is customary, so the tyranny of rationalism tends to preempt reason, itself. Since the break-up of the medieval synthesis under the impact of science, capitalism, and mass civilization, even individuals of the Western world have sometimes experienced such a sense of powerlessness that "fear of freedom" has prepared a way for Big Brother.[105] As we know, the slogans of Orwell's *1984*--"Peace is War" and "Freedom is Slavery"--reveal insanity at the core of purely logical formulations.

Although the concept of the *un*-conscious mind--related to spontaneity, intuition, and imagination--has been available since ancient times, Descartes thrust it down in favor of the alpine air of logic and deductive reasoning.

Now, the rediscovery of the unconscious mind is of the highest interest in our consideration of the problem of human survival. The human "mind" is, if limited to rational consciousness, prepared to wrap the whole planet in a shroud, and the exercise of all our best efforts and ingenuity has produced no assurance that it will be deterred from that end. Moreover, the prolonged failure of purely rational consciousness in dealing with world crisis simply points to its inadequacy, to the need for transcending them in a fresh approach. This is the promise of imagination; it has power to effect alteration of our inner life and of the outer forms in which life finds expression and support. Imagination can break up too rigid patterns of thought and feeling and shape them to meet the needs of life. Imagination gives psychological, empathic presence to the absent, which can be the not-self, even the mass of the earth's inhabitants. Imagination, when externalized as a creative product, is changed to relate to reality by means of a conceptualizing component. Our ability to conceptualize exposes us to an unending organization of cognitive elements, an unending variety of emotions, and the possibility of moral choice. Man is a product not simply of nature, but also of his own making.

A friend of mine who taught briefly at a university in the former Soviet Union summed up his impressions in three words: "Skinnerism. No fun." Depressing as that picture is, we might lift--and lengthen--our gaze to envision ourselves not as doomed automatons, but as creatures in a stage of evolving World Culture. The creative imagination envisions vast social implications. A creative society uncovers, selects, reshuffles, combines, and synthesizes already existing facts, ideas, faculties, and skills. By contrast, a closed society will decay for lack of exchanges with an unceasing expansion of reality. In the monotonous environment of a closed society, responses will become stereotyped, flexible skills will degenerate into rigid patterns, and the person will more and more resemble an automaton governed by fixed habits.

The spiritual determinant of World Culture has been and can continue to be the individual. If I read correctly the teachings of Jesus, world peace begins with personal peace—Gnostic "Oneness" or the radical transformation of atonement. The technological determinant of World Culture has been, at an accelerating pace since the twelfth century A.D., the methods of science, and so we can put our knowledge to use in a responsible way with individual consciousness, not monumental mythological authorities, as the actual center of awe and hope.

As I began with borrowing the wisdom of Joseph Campbell, so I shall conclude. In the long view, we see a gradual amplification of the group from the early tribal cluster to the modern concept of a single World Culture. Against the amplitude of this concept, the various national, racial, religious or class mythologies that may once have had their authority are now being replaced by inter-thinking globalists. In the recent past it may have been possible for intelligent men of good will honestly to believe that their own society was the only good, that beyond its bounds were the enemies of God, and that they were called upon, consequently, to project the principle of hatred outward upon the world, while cultivating love within those whose system of belief was of God. Today, however, physical facts have made closed horizons illusory. The old god of little, closed societies is dead. "There are today no horizons, no mythogenetic zones," Campbell writes. "Or rather, the mythogenetic zone is the individual heart . . . each the creative center of authority for himself."[106] Our task is to awaken within each of us the principle of love as it was mythologically wakened in God. *No man is an island. Every man is a piece of the continent.* Mythology, too, functions to initiate the individual into the order of realities of his own psyche, guiding him toward his own spiritual enrichment and realization. Formerly--but in archaic cultures still--the way was to subordinate all individual judgment, will, and capacities to the social order. Gradually in Europe, the principle of individual judgment and responsibility was developed in relation not to a fixed order of supposed divine laws, but to a changing context of human activities, rationally governed. This humanistic individualism has released powers of imagination that have revolutionized the world and set the task for each of us to integrate the fire within into our quest for those values by which cultural sterility is redeemed.

The full emergence of a new world of consciousness is yet to come, but it is already far enough advanced as to give us hope for survival. Our laws are from ourselves, not from the gods or from the universe; they are conventional, not absolute; and in breaking them we offend our fellow human beings and our fragile planet. We, ourselves, elicit the sense of awe before the mystery of being, and we support that sense with a cosmology based upon the discoveries of the arts and sciences in the depths of both the psyche and the galaxies of space. *Involved in mankind*, we have by nature essentially and by the accident of nuclear technology necessarily the power to be at-one with all others. Man, of course, is not an end in himself in an absolute sense. He has not created the universe or himself. He has, however, employed imagination to create all cultures and, pretending otherwise, authorized war. He no longer has that self-appointed authority because war, as an expression of cultures, no longer functions mythologically. In order to abolish war and to survive, he emphatically does not need, as is sometimes argued, to change human nature. He needs to change his bad habits. He needs the circles of his love to expand, like the ever-widening ripples on a pond, to include the mutual humanity of all the other selves here and now and to come, in each and all. And he will, I think, fulfill those needs, given patience and fortitude to persevere and vigilance to protect his ever-larger sky from the last trumpets of his own folly.

CHAPTER 10

A Coming World of Consciousness

Not long ago some groups of young white males openly identifying themselves as neo-Nazis and white supremacists rallied in Charlottesville, Virginia, supposedly to protest the planned removal of a statue of Robert E. Lee, the Confederate general. Alerted to this invasion of their quiet and lovely town, famed the world over as the place where Thomas Jefferson lived at nearby Monticello and where he founded The University of Virginia, citizens of all ages, rank, and racial identities confronted the groups with the most Jeffersonian of values, eternal vigilance against every form of tyranny over the mind of man. A pasty-faced, arctic-eyed terrorist plowed his car into the crowd, killing a young woman named Heather Heyer. In remembrance of the death of that young woman, I want to summon up, in the spirit of love for a person I never knew, the vision of a triumph over the darkness in our souls.

But first let me admit to some shame about my own family heritage. My forebears were Southern and Northern, slaveowners and racists in the mix with abolitionists and intrepid humanitarians. Although I was born and raised in Durham, North Carolina, and attended segregated public schools there through ninth grade, I preferred the company of King Arthur and his Knights of the Round Table to that of my Southern kin, most of whom I considered as out of their minds. My father's parents, who had been missionaries in Persia and believed in the literal truth of the Bible, raised their family in small Upcountry South Carolina towns where the Lord was supposed to provide but didn't, and there in the fiefdom of John C. Calhoun, they prided themselves as his descendants, though the linkage is extremely vague. The desire to be identified with a slave-owning Vice-President and the virtual grandfather of the Confederacy is no consummation to be wished, devoutly or otherwise. Grandma Amy's mother, Malvina Black Gist Waring, is nowadays actually hailed in South Carolina for having been an incorrigibly defiant Reb, even at one time a treasurer of the Confederacy. She was a valiant lady who wrote romances and hated "Yankees." True, her first husband, Major Gist, had been killed in a skirmish the day before Shiloh, and her second husband had been humiliated along with others who surrendered the city of Columbia to General Sherman. But all that was gone with the wind. For good measure I'll throw into the record of remembering Time my other grandfather, Hugh Bayne of New Orleans whose father, a Confederate officer, amused himself by wrestling with his slaves. "Colonel," as he liked to be called, kept a Confederate flag in his digs in a Yale retirement facility in New Haven. I can cringe about that bit of lunacy, but I can't excuse his insulting of Levi Jackson, the pioneering black Captain of the Yale football team of 1948. Levi was also a star of the basketball team to which I was a freshman apprentice, a skinny 6'3" and 160 pounds with a hook shot. One afternoon on the bus to West Point to play Army, Levi sat next to me and spoke as if I were a kid brother. Now, traditionally, Skull and Bones, the secret Yale society beloved by Colonel, tapped football captains for membership, so when I learned that Colonel was distributing in the streets of New Haven and halls of Yale College some leaflets proclaiming, in effect, that Levi was not a legitimate "brother" for Skull & Bones, I was shocked and embarrassed to a degree I'd never experienced before. It is one thing to joke about kinfolk being out of their minds, another to realize that one's liberal Yankee mother's own father was *evil*.

The literary imagination paid me, when I was seventeen-years-old at Phillips Academy Andover, an extraordinary visit and wouldn't leave consciousness until I'd written a sketch about a stranger. He and a little boy were encountering one another down by a river. The boy, who lived in a nearby farmhouse, had been skipping stones on the water while the stranger, an old mixed-blood Negro Indian, had been fishing. I, of course, was that boy, and the river was the Eno about ten miles from Durham, but the dark-skinned stranger must have emanated from the unconscious spirit of place. He had no recognizable affiliation with any person I'd ever known. North of Boston, perhaps 600 miles away from home, I wasn't reading or thinking about race beyond the fact that an Indian tribe, driven by the British out of Virginia, had settled in the Eno River region in the seventeenth century.

The promptings of the imagination that reach consciousness represent, I believe, the inherent desire of the spirit to be whole. Seventy years have passed since Christopher Stebbins, an imaginary boy, met Wesley Jackson, an imaginary man who incorporated, as it were, centuries of genocide and slavery. Seventy years ago, though I knew it not, there was for me in the personage of a Negro Indian an Other who had been assimilated into my spiritual whole.

You, Heather Heyer, were, having assimilated peoples of the Earth into consciousness, spiritually whole.

Who killed Heather Heyer? There was a hate-filled assailant with a terror-car for a weapon. There were the groups of neo-Nazis and white supremacists who deliberately provoked courageous Americans to defend democracy and the honor of our land. The answer to the question about Heather Heyer's death goes far and deeply beyond the matter of Who. The answer ultimately lies in the Where and the What. Although the murder took place in Charlottesville, it actually occurred in every town, every city, every part of America unless there is some location where hearts harbor no darkness. Violence is everywhere. We come to what actually caused the death of this young woman: *race-fear*. And once we swallow the fact that American life is and always has been permeated by race-fear, we at last begin to envision the possibility of creating and living in a world without it. Heather Heyer was sacrificed for a future of inter-connected, inter-thinking humanity.

In that real world of possibility, we already have scientific evidence from genetic structures that we are all of us connected. We are all of us brothers and sisters. There is no such a thing as racial purity. There are no divinely sanctioned peoples and places to support the concept of divided humankind.

You, Heather Heyer, exemplify the higher levels consciousness that endow the literary imagination with the authority to lift our hearts in memory of a person in the vanguard of a new world of the mind.

Should I return now to the subject of literary imagination?

It is quite possible that publication and perpetuity didn't matter very much to Edward de Vere. While it's true that some of his sonnets claim immortality for what he is writing, he could hardly have believed he had thus conquered Time and Death. In fact, the convention that one's poetry will last for a long period of time seems, when he indulges in it, unconvincing. Is literary immortality really all he has to offer the person he loves?

That Edward de Vere, Earl of Oxford, was the man who was "Shakespeare" is nowadays, for an increasing number of scholars and dramatists, pretty much a proven fact. Why would one of the world's greatest poets and dramatists usurp another man's name if he really desires an after-death notoriety? While as yet we have no clear answer to the question, we can make a guess: Queen Elizabeth, who was fond of de Vere, had a chopping block ready to receive the head of any aristocrat who stepped out of line and displeased her. He could risk flattering her with *Venus and Adonis* and *Lucrece*, but to write plays for the masses and impregnate these and sonnets with humanistic imagination without submission to religious dogmatism might well, I surmise, have proven fatal. Let him duck behind conventional insincerity. Better yet, let him be an imposter whose true identity is known only to a few others, Ben Jonson, for example.[107]

Whatever the reason for perpetrating a hoax, one which deceives the world to this day, some of de Vere's sonnets are inadequate responses to the prospect of death. Here from Sonnet 19 are typical lines of the kind:

> Yet do thy worst, old Time: despite thy wrong
> My love shall in my verse ever live young.

Now compare and contrast Sonnet 19 with Sonnet 65 with its reference to the imaginative miracle of "black ink" as the poet's real idea of what is lasting about his celebration of love:

> unless this miracle have might,
> That in black ink my love may still shine bright.

Here in Sonnet 65 is profound awareness of a poet's "miracle" to which written poetry, though necessary, is subsidiary. G. Wilson Knight, the great Shakespearean scholar, unveils the true meaning of these lines: "The poet knows that through his poetry, or the poetic consciousness, he establishes, or focuses, a supernatural reality, or truth, what we may call a 'poetic dimension,' that cannot otherwise be attained." What matters is not perpetuity but a universal principle that Knight calls "a state-of-being, or dimension, which can be thought of variously as infinite time or as timelessness." Knight sums up his interpretation not only of the sonnet but also, I think, of imaginative literature in general by saying that it "enjoys an authority, or exists from a dimension, to which all temporal fabrication and engagements are as nothing."[108]

Shakespeare's use of the word "miracle" refers to a supernal power, not, as is common today, to something merely remarkable like a "miracle drug." In Sonnet 107 he conveys his sense of the miraculous as also a force in history:

> Not mine own fears, nor the prophetic soul,
> Of the wide world, dreaming on things to come,
> Can yet the lease of my true love control,
> Supposed as forfeit to a confined doom.
> The mortal moon hath her eclipse endured,
> And the sad augurs mock their own presage,
> Uncertainties now crown themselves assured,
> And peace proclaims olives of endless age.

Until Leslie Hotson's connecting of the poem and historical events came along, these lines were considered the most difficult in all of the *Sonnets*. I follow his elucidation of them. The metaphor of an eclipsed moon refers to the defeated Spanish Armada. Shakespeare is celebrating that turning-point, the year 1588 in history. For more than a century Europeans had expected 1588 to be a day of doom, the fall of England a prophecy which spread alarm and led to a belief that "doom" would put a "confine," a limit or end, to the life of the world. But the invincible Armada has suffered defeat! Instead of cataclysm, 1588 has brought to England, and to all Protestant Europe with her, the certain assurance of peace.[109]

Doom having been eclipsed and peace assured, the sonnet's tone, though playful, is still for the most part subdued, even humble. While "the prophetic soul… dreaming on things to come" has failed to predict victory, its importance has not been diminished. The visionary power of the human imagination is to be regarded as a necessary endowment even though it may seem to lack the force of control associated with a miraculous intervention in history. Indeed, literature has always been accommodating to prophecy, albeit visionaries themselves may initially seem to be so far ahead of their times as to be mocked or ignored as mystics with no feet on the ground. Future-shockers such as Aldous Huxley's *Brave New World* and George Orwell's *1984* are fables cleverly extrapolated in a mathematical figure from already known values, whereas the truly visionary work of art comes out of the depths. Whatever the temporal limitation of our wide world, there is in imagination a potential for effecting unpredicted change. The speaker in Shakespeare's sonnet, fearful of permanent confinement, has nevertheless implicitly, like an American slave before the Emancipation Proclamation, endured by *imagining* freedom! The trick of fate has not been precisely predictable, but humanity has the ability to see around corners.

In 1965 when I was teaching creative writing at the University of Pennsylvania in Philadelphia, I had the good fortune to make the acquaintance of Ralph Ellison. Assigned by the Department of English to accompany him as he was making his rounds of appointments, I soon found that the author of *Invisible Man*, a novel (composed 1945-1952) I greatly admired, was easy to get along with, soft-spoken, an artist so poised as seldom to allow himself to show surprise or be upset.

One morning after I met him at the department, we walked together across lawns to have lunch at a small restaurant on Walnut Street. It was February 21, 1965.

I need exposition here: one of the most powerful moments in *Invisible Man* comes when a charismatic young organizer of the Brotherhood in New York, Brother Tod Clifton, is assassinated by a policeman:

> At first, I thought it was a cop and a shoeshine boy; then there was a break in the traffic and across the sun-glaring bands of trolley rails I recognized Clifton. His partner had disappeared now, and Clifton had the box slung to his left shoulder with the cop moving slowly behind and to one side of him. They were coming my way, passing a newsstand, and I saw the rails in the asphalt and a fire plug at the curb and the flying birds, and thought, You'll have to follow and pay his fine… just as the cop pushed him, jolting him forward and Clifton trying to keep the box from swinging against his leg and saying something over his shoulder and going forward as one of the pigeons swung down into the street and up again, leaving a feather floating white in the dazzling backlight of the sun, and I could see the cop push Clifton again, stepping solidly forward in his black shirt, his arm shooting out stiffly, sending him in a head-snapping forward stumble until he caught himself, saying something over his shoulder again, the two moving in a kind of march that I'd seen many times, but never with anyone like Clifton. And I could see the cop bark a command and lunge forward, thrusting out his arm and missing, thrown off balance as suddenly Clifton spun on his toes like a dancer

and swung his right arm over and around in a short, jolting arc, his torso carrying forward and to the left in a motion that sent the box strap free as his right foot traveled forward and his left arm followed through in a floating uppercut that sent the cop's cap sailing into the street and his feet flying, to drop him hard, rocking from left to right on the walk as Clifton kicked the box thudding aside and crouched, his left foot forward, his hands high, waiting. And between the flashing of cars I could see the cop propping himself on his elbows like a drunk trying to get his head up, shaking it and thrusting it forward — And somewhere between the dull roar of traffic and the subway vibrating underground I heard rapid explosions and saw each pigeon diving wildly as though blackjacked by the sound, and the cop sitting up straight now, and rising to his knees looking steadily at Clifton, and the pigeons plummeting swiftly into trees, and Clifton still facing the cop and suddenly crumpling.[110]

As Ellison and I were about to eat, a student rushed into the restaurant and cried out almost hysterically, "Malcolm X has been assassinated! Malcolm X has been assassinated!" Startled and with an inward awareness of many things at once—the assassination of President Kennedy little more than year earlier, Malcolm X as a charismatic young black leader, the scene in *Invisible Man* quoted above—I turned to Ellison. His countenance reflected no alarm. I said "Tod Clifton, Mr. Ellison! Tod Clifton. You predicted years ago what has just happened!"

"No," Ellison said quietly after a pause. "If you work at a certain depth of imagination, you are bound to anticipate future events, but you never know in advance what those are going to be."

What if spirituality, the feeling of transcendence, is genetically based? What if we have an innate capacity for spirituality and that the desire to reach out beyond oneself, which is at the heart of the literary imagination, is part of the human makeup? *People can abandon or change that which culture, history, and environment may have determined for them, thanks to imagination and, possibly, a genetic propensity for spirituality. And this spirituality can be built on and developed through creative arts such as literature.* The ability to lose one's sense of self, to become at-one with the universe and everybody and everything in it, is essential to human survival. Spirituality is based in consciousness, of which imagination is a part, while everything that is not from nature is, in a sense, a story or a fiction, cultures, religions, all that.

Dean Hamer sees consciousness as key to peace, understanding, and compassion.[111] Accordingly, I would argue, imaginative literature, far from being "elitist" or irrelevant, is indicative of everything we must take seriously. No simple word or phrase for this power of consciousness is completely satisfactory. What Hamer calls "spirituality" has to be distinguished from "religion." Knight's concept of a "dimension" of "timelessness" will be somewhat off-putting for those who object to "mysticism" and New Age meditation, not to mention Carl Jung's theory of synchronicity, meaningful coincidences outside time as we know it. Knight's "poetic consciousness" will sound effete and even repugnant in our excessively rationalistic and materialistic culture, and "imagination" and "fantasy" and "invention" differ in meaning. *Imagination* nevertheless remains the compelling term. It is the power to which I refer metaphorically as *the fire within*, "fire" suggesting a visionary driving force in one's life and work. We can defend literature—and vocational study of and participation in it—as giving us a sense of sanctuary in a coming world of consciousness.

"Soon enough," Naomi Klein writes in *This Changes Everything*, "no one will be safe from the sorrow of ecocide." We have allowed ourselves to be brought to this existential crisis by hubris, the excessive arrogance, I won't resist mentioning, identified for our civilization since ancient times in great literature. Aeschylus, Sophocles, and Euripides feared hubristic tyrants for ignoring the very values by means of which people should govern their lives. The ancient Greeks perceived that ignorance brought on catastrophe. Today the fall of our House is not that of a dynasty but that of the human species. In spite of evidence that unfettered capitalism has some responsibility for climate change, Klein argues, the "empathy-exterminating mind-set" of a few persuades them that they "are still masters of the universe" and that, after all, "we are nothing but selfish, greedy, self-gratification machines" who are "fundamentally not worth saving."[112]

Since climate change changes everything, and our moral character is being tested as never before, why are we not setting out deliberately and immediately to rely upon consciousness to strengthen values that are currently being vindicated by the laws of nature?

Chris Hedges in *Empire of Illusion* (2009) gives a withering account of our paralysis. A "cult of distraction," he writes, "masks the real disintegration of culture . . . conceals the meaninglessness and emptiness of our own lives" and "seduces us to engage in imitative consumption," deflecting "the moral questions arising from mounting social injustice, growing inequalities, costly imperial wars, economic collapse, and political corruption."[113] At the core of Hedges's disenchantment with the America he loves is the prospect of an end of literacy.

> We are a culture that has been denied, or has passively given up, the linguistic and intellectual tools to cope with complexity, to separate illusion from reality. We have traded the printed word for the gleaming image. Public rhetoric is designed to be comprehensible to a ten-year-old child or an adult with a sixth-grade reading level. Most of us speak at this level, are entertained and think at this level. We have transformed our culture into a vast replica of Pinocchio's Pleasure Island, where boys were lured with the promise of no school and endless fun. They were all, however, turned into donkeys—a symbol, in Italian culture, of ignorance and stupidity. Functional illiteracy in North America is epidemic. There are 7 million illiterate Americans. Another 27 million are unable to read well enough to complete a job application, and 30 million can't read a simple sentence. There are some 50 million who read at a fourth- or fifth-grade level. Nearly a third of the nation's population is illiterate or barely literate—a figure that is growing by more than 2 million a year. A third of high-school graduates never read another book for the rest of their lives, and neither do 42 percent of college graduates. In 2007, 80 percent of the families in the United States did not buy or read a book. And it is not much better beyond our borders. Canada has an illiterate and semiliterate population estimated at 42 percent of the whole, a proportion that mirrors that of the United States.[114]

The end of literacy fosters a flight into illusion:

> The use of pseudo-events to persuade rather than overtly brainwash renders millions of us unable to see or question the structures and systems that are impoverishing us and, in some cases, destroying our lives. The flight into illusion sweeps away the core values of the open society. It corrodes the ability to think for oneself, to draw independent conclusions, to express dissent when judgment and common sense tell you something is wrong, to be self-critical, to challenge authority, to grasp historical facts, to advocate for change, and to acknowledge that there are other views, different ways, and structures of being that are morally and socially acceptable. A populace deprived of the ability to separate

lies from truth, that has become hostage to the fictional semblance of reality put forth by pseudo-events, is no longer capable of sustaining a free society.[115]

Finally, Hedges warns, assault against the humanities is sealing us off from the way to a new world of consciousness:

> The bankruptcy of our economic and political systems can be traced directly to the assault against the humanities. The neglect of the humanities has allowed elites to organize education and society around predetermined answers to predetermined questions. Students are taught structures designed to produce these answers even as these structures have collapsed. But those in charge, because they are educated only in specializations designed to maintain these economic and political structures, have run out of ideas. They have been trained only to find solutions that will maintain the system. That is what the Harvard Business School case method is about, a didactic system in which the logic employed to solve a specific problem always, in the end, sustains market capitalism. These elites are not capable of asking the broad, universal questions, the staples of an education in the humanities, which challenge the deepest assumptions of a culture and examine the harsh realities of political and economic power. They have forgotten, because they have not been taught, that human nature is a mixture of good and evil. They do not have the capacity for critical reflection. They do not understand that for every answer there arises another question—the very basis behind the Socratic academy's search for wisdom.[116]

The subtitle of *Empire of Illusion* is *The End of Literacy and the Triumph of Spectacle*. It's a perfect summing-up of what is happening in America today, the political situation in particular.

We have forgotten, too, perhaps because we have not been taught, that imagination has been *central* to the history of humankind. Yuval Noah Harari's *Sapiens: A Brief History of Humankind* forcefully reminds us of this centrality. While constrained by biology and physics, our species coexists in imaginary worlds of its own devising. Fictions foster social cooperation and rapid cultural evolution, promoting our outstanding ability to adapt and innovate. Legends, myths, gods and religions appeared for the first time about 20,000 years ago. Imagination enabled us not merely to talk about entire entities that do not exist at all, but to do so collectively.

Every Sapiens band continued to run its life independently and provide for most of its needs. An archaic sociologist living 20,000 years ago . . . might well have concluded that mythology had a fairly limited scope. Stories about ancestral spirits and tribal totems were strong enough to enable 500 people to trade seashells, celebrate the odd festival, and join forces to wipe out a Neanderthal band, but no more than that. Mythology, the ancient sociologist would have thought, could not possibly enable millions of strangers to cooperate on a daily basis.

But that turned out to be wrong. Myths, it transpired, are stronger than anyone could have imagined. When the Agricultural Revolution opened opportunities for the creation of crowded cities and mighty empires, people invented stories about the great gods, motherlands and joint stock companies to provide the needed social links. While human evolution was crawling at its usual snail's pace, the human imagination was building astounding networks of mass cooperation, unlike any other ever seen on earth. [117]

Our present cultural malaise and ecological concerns, seen in this light, are not inevitably doom-laden. In spite of centuries during which Western culture has been suspicious of the imagination, defining it as inferior to reason, what Harari is presenting simply as "stories" are actually redemptive, perhaps in the nick of Earth's time. The very survival of humankind and the natural world, I repeat, depends upon our ability to adapt and innovate. The power for this ability is the fire within.

If we shift from the study of literature to neuropsychology, this redemptive vision of a coming world of consciousness can be shown to be rooted in the way the mind actually works.

Few people, I surmise, really believe in the possibility of peace, though most would profess an abhorrence of war and assert that they, themselves, are pacific with but occasional outbursts of aggressive behavior, usually justified on the basis that human beings are, after all, animals. Peace is a dream, an ideal, whereas war seems the natural state for the species, consequently inevitable and unavoidable. Pointing to history, we observe the violent rise and fall of civilizations. We conclude that civilization is doomed, with it, all mankind. If anything is to save us, we deceive ourselves into thinking, it is technology. We need to open our eyes and see not Star Wars but Peace Stars.

Our awareness of peaceful possibility is, to borrow an analogy, a little like our ability to see stars in daytime. The sun is so bright that the stars are invisible, despite the fact that they are just as present in our sky in the daytime as at night. When the sun sets, we are able to perceive the stars. In the same way, the brilliance of our most recent evolutionary accretion, the analytical, verbal, and "scientific" abilities of human consciousness, obscures our awareness of the cognitive functions of the intuitive, integrative, and holistic abilities of human consciousness, which in our ancestors must have been the principal means of perceiving the world. In fact, when it is a question of human survival, imagination may actually be the most competent mode of awareness, with our highly prized rational and analytical abilities quite ineffective, unless collaborating with intuition, to solve complex problems. We already possess, in other words, the Peace Stars that can save us and our plundered planet. They do not sparkle in outer space. Instead, the new world of the future lies in the interstellar spaces within ourselves where the creative fire dwells.

How, we might well ask, did we get into our daytime blindness? The ideology of the modern world, by which I mean chiefly Western civilization, has been derived from some crucial misconceptions about the nature of the mind, itself. Since the rise of modern science in the seventeenth century and as a consequence of Cartesian and Lockean theories of rationalism, "mind" has been regarded as synonymous with reason, and all other effects and processes of thinking have been relegated to a distasteful, demonic, and useless black box, the unconscious. But rationalism—or, to be more precise, *over*-rationalism—has not been the only fallacious assumption in the civilization of the recent West. Materialism is another. Under the materialistic assumption, mind and matter are separated, so that the material universe, be it seas, forests, or atomic particles, exists for our "property," our personal use, exploitation, and enrichment without any social regard for such emotional and spiritual sentiments as the sanctity of an environment that nourishes life. That both rationalism and materialism, for all their advances, have brought us to the brink of catastrophe, we in our blindness are still not quite ready to admit. We forget that John Locke made reason the only permitted source of spiritual being in individuals and thus severed any organic relation which makes an individual dependent upon the existence of other persons. Locke gave low status to emotions and passions. People exhibiting these and proclaiming the priority of human rights over property rights are, in a tendency of Western ideology, regarded as inferior and unrealistic. This category of the ideologically weak includes poets, artists, women, and most of the world's so-called primal and nonscientific populations.

But is there really a coming world of consciousness? Will it be a consciousness expanded into the form of world understanding, ecological preservation, and peace? There is a remarkable and increasing amount of evidence that the answers to these fundamental questions are in the affirmative.

Over millions of years, the human species has been in process of becoming until we are now conscious of our existence in three-dimensional space (length, breadth, height) and in three-dimensional time (past, present, future). However, this three-dimensional sense of time is expanding into a fourth dimension, an "apperception" released from the unconscious psychic forces to unite us with eternity. As we perceive ourselves as part of the mysterious unity and continuity of life, our encounter with timelessness may evoke beneficent psychical energy. If we maintain our psyche's balance with the evolutionary way that the Native Americans have always mythologized as Emergence on the Road of Life, we will emerge to a stage of increased awareness with an ethic of earthly preservation and human solidarity.

Evidently, we are just starting to come out of our Cartesian-Lockean swoon and to learn that we are future-oriented beings who, early in life, can make automatic and habitual the actions that serve peace through unity of mind and brain.

The automatism of habit as a derivative of consciousness has dynamic implications. Psychologist David Klein gives a simple illustration of how balked habits reinstate alertness to the conditions responsible for their frustration.

> The experienced driver can be absorbed in conversation with a passenger while the automatism of habit permits him to act as a quasi-mechanical chauffeur. He gives focal attention to the ideas being exchanged and only peripheral or subliminal attention to the engine and the road. This holds true as long as the situation is routine, but there is immediate and drastic reversal in the face of engine failure or hazardous road conditions, which precipitate maximum attention to the business of driving. If the engine fails, a veteran driver will stop the car at the side of the highway, as he will do if he hears a fire siren or sees an ambulance approaching. This is a commonplace maneuver for experienced drivers and becomes an inherent component of their entrenched driving habits, executed through force of habit.[118]

What is especially striking about the dynamics of persistent motivation, Klein concludes, is their ethical implications for the development of desirable traits of character and the reaping of the destiny of nations from the sowing of such traits. The nervous system can be our ally instead of our enemy.

Such conclusions from the field of psychology become compelling when we move to the field of neuropsychology to study neurons, the highly specialized cells that comprise the elementary units of the central nervous system. Unlike other cells in the body, neurons—and this is their magic—are modifiable. They change as the result of growth during development and maturation—and they change as the result of experience.

Let us now peer into the black box.

As our eyes become accustomed to the dark and our metaphorical telescope is trained on the interstellar spaces of the brain, we discern—of course figuratively speaking—a constellation of marvelous stars becoming ever brighter in our time and bearing auspicious tidings of the mind's ability to understand itself. These are, let us say, Peace Stars, and the wonder aroused by discovery prompts me, a nonscientist, to alter their abstract names into strange, poetic ones, like powers of a galactic allegory: Hemisphaeria is a bright star, Callosum is brighter still, Cognon is absolutely brilliant, and Heterarkia may yet prove most radiant of all.

Hemisphaeria, the star that has been known since ancient times in the concept of duality, loomed into recent view with discovery by Nobel-Prize-winning psychologist-physiologist Roger W. Sperry of right and left hemispheres of the brain, with lateral specialization of function to each hemisphere but also with some doubling of conscious awareness. At first, the powerful evidence that our left brain is specialized for language led investigators to call this the "dominant" hemisphere, implying that the right side of the brain was subordinate, minor, and inferior. But such one-sided emphasis on language, perhaps our most distinctive human characteristic, allowed us to overlook the extremely important spatial, attentional, emotional, and musical abilities that are possessed by the nontalking half of the human brain. The mistake was to concentrate on cognitive functions related to intelligence, perception, language, verbal learning, and memory, and to pay little attention to expressive and receptive aspects of emotion. Not until it was realized that emotions and feelings are also localizable has the mistake been rectified. Now there is dramatic proof that affective aspects of language are localized in specific parts of the right hemisphere of the brain. As Alberta Gilinsky reports in *Mind and*

Brain, "the findings on emotional processes do not support the idea that one side of the brain is rational, intellectual, or cognitive, in contrast to an impulsive, affective, or emotional side. Instead, both hemispheres possess affective aspects, but the right and left hemispheres have different emotional response patterns."[119] The idea of duality, of two brains that influence development, is a striking one and explains some of our inner conflicts. For example, we may believe strongly in peace, ecological preservation, and equality for all, yet thrill to war, to the slaughter of whales, and to exclusion of women and minorities from the economic and political arena. Evidently, we need two brains, each hemisphere providing space for increasing specializations of functions, but we also need a fusion to take place at the midline to knit the two hemispheres together and, by uniting them, actually increase our powers of mind.

The star Callosum does exactly this. It is, of course, the Corpus Callosum, the bundle of nerve fibers which is the principal cabling between left and right hemispheres of the cerebral cortex. When Carl Sagan declares that "The path to the future lies through the corpus callosum," he is seeing a coming world of consciousness.[120] As we now know that the brain has evolved to the point of connecting its two hemispheres, it is clear that we possess the capacity for combining critical thinking with creative and intuitive insights in a coordinated search for new patterns. We have simply underestimated this capacity and doomed ourselves to sterility and possible annihilation.

I have said that the star Cognon is absolutely brilliant. Here's why. In 1972 a group of investigators at Princeton University were studying the cortex in macaque monkeys when a particularly stubborn neuron was encountered from which the investigators were unable to elicit any response, no matter what stimulus they tried. Finally, one of them began to wave his hand in front of one monkey's eyes. Immediately the reluctant neuron sprang into an excited burst of activity. What was the cell responding to? For the next twelve hours, the investigators tested the cell's response to one silhouette after another—symmetrical patterns, five-pointed stars, leaf patterns, a cut-out of the human hand, and, finally, a cardboard model of the monkey's own paw. That stimulus evoked the most vigorous response. Thus, it was deduced that a biologically meaningful stimulus object is importantly represented in the cognitive field of the monkey's brain. Hence, we can postulate what Gilinsky, synthesizing psychology and neurophysiology into a unified field of neuropsychology, calls the "cognon," an elementary unit of thought derived from perceptual learning but constrained by the prewired cellular structure of the brain. As our brains have developed by superimposing on primitive layers the new layers of cortical integration, multiple new cognons have formed in minicolumns (about five million of them in turn composed of about 60-billion nerve cells) to represent all experienced objects and patterns and to provide the serial order in thought and action. The most fascinating aspect of the cognon is its ability to "call up" an image in anticipation of an expected event. As we undergo new experiences, cognons form to represent them. The mind has the capacity for permanently changing its structure by interacting with the environment. As we learn new patterns of behavior, we can retain the change permanently and irreversibly. Cognon's star quality is precisely this: "As cognons are formed in the cognitive centers of the brain, they . . . take part in providing the stimuli for still higher-order cognons."[121]

Gilinsky illustrates the role that mind may play in changing our notions of reality by asking us to consider the word "grandfather." A grandfather is simply the father of a parent. Yet he must be old, bent, bespectacled, bearded, of beaming wrinkles and gentle ways. So it comes as a shock to you to learn that your car-racing friend with his smooth young face is a grandfather. Does your image of grandfather change? Not at all. What is most likely to change is that your grandfather stereotype remains in one set of cognons just as before, but now you make room for a new set of cognons representing youthful, daring grandfathers. The new set does not replace the old set. Instead, you now have two sets of related but independent cognons in place of one.[122]

Certainly, some such process is currently changing our notions of "feminine" and "masculine" behavior even as we cling to old gender stereotypes. This process must be awakening us to the notion, an ancient one, of Earth as our nurturing Mother who must be preserved, even as we cling to stereotypes of Earth as exploitable matter. Evolution has given the mammalian brain its competitive edge by introducing into its activity a flexible, integrative thrust, with lower-level cognons forming higher-order cognons.

Here coming into astonishing, unexpected focus of our metaphorical telescope is the great star *Heterarkia* which represents the flexibility of organization that explains the superiority of the human brain. We have, according to Gilinsky, three pictures of the mind's architecture. One is that programs are combined serially, data from one program taken over by the next in line—always a linear, assembly line progression of neural reactions. Another picture is that the combination occurs hierarchically, with one program having overall control and the flow of control moving from top down. Neither system has flexibility, for both assembly line and hierarchy suffer from the fixed progression of responsibility through successive levels of the system. The heterarchical arrangement offers equal distribution of responsibility for control throughout the system. Gilinsky, who compares the brain's architecture to a smoothly functioning football team, concludes:

> Our heterarchical brain is a dynamically organized, interconnected set of systems and subsystems that can pass control from one to another in many different directions. Earlier units in a heterarchy can be modified by the activity of the later ones, later units can undo mistakes, and units at any point can forestall adverse contingencies. This is the power of intelligence responsible for the higher reaches of human thought.[123]

This image of the central nervous system as a heterarchy should give pause to those whose model for world order is a hierarchy. A heterarchy achieves orderliness by having many autonomous units serving in specialized capacities on different levels of the system and brings all units to work toward common goals through harmony, mutual respect, and unity of purpose.

We have gazed at Peace Stars but have not named the constellation of which they are a part—Consciousness. As it happens, no line can be drawn between conscious and unconscious "sides" of the brain: all neural structures are involved in the programming and guidance of behavior. In carrying out the survival function of the nervous system, evolution must have favored the development of consciousness, allowing us, when we are confronted with increasingly complex, changing environments, to call for radically different adaptations and for selection of appropriate actions. Consciousness plays a causal role in brain function and behavior. Gilinsky sums up this role of consciousness, as follows:

> Complex work involving millions of neurons and billions of synapses takes place at a level that proceeds effectively without our conscious intervention. Consciousness is thus freed to concentrate on the priorities of the moment, and by its selective emphasis can direct our behavior to our self-selected ends.[124]

Such a view of consciousness represents to the neuropsychologist a revolution in our conception of the nature of intelligence. The cardinal virtue of imagination, let us remember, is freedom. The literary imagination, I suspect, has known about this "revolution" for thousands of years.

As we stand on the threshold of a new epoch, there are indeed signs betokening the emergence from the unconscious of those contents that, unified with conscious elements, will lead to a union of the opposite polarities. Already we are psychically beginning our transition to a new world of consciousness. If world crisis prompts us, as seems possible, to recover spiritual wholeness, our fire within will of itself help us to control our drive toward annihilation.

Our evolving consciousness, in all probability a hardwired one with an innate capacity to love, must combat our own auguries of dread. In a timely and sublime growth out of our currently marginalized idea of imagination, we will, I believe, be delivered of temporal engagements of the old order, and a new world of consciousness may emerge. Doomsayers hope for sudden up-risings and movements, and such acts of political power may occur, but they will be preceded by what is inherent in us all, experienced especially by mythmakers, poets, and writers. The fire within, the compelling and irresistible inner drive of all humankind, the miracle of our imagination, is our sanctuary of hope. What is valid in the fire might extend its validity by inseminating the consciousness of others for whom vision has failed, thus helping to create a new world out of the wreckage of the modern age since the Industrial Revolution. To understand what our imagination is up to and to find hope in the imagination in action is a calling with an ancestry of noble purpose and a vision quest of genuine spiritual promise.

NOTES

[1]"We are today as far into the electric age as the Elizabethans had advanced into the typographical and mechanical age. And we are experiencing the same confusions and indecisions which they felt when living simultaneously in two contrasted forms of society and experience." Marshall McLuhan, *The Gutenberg Galaxy: The Making of Typographic Man* (Toronto: University of Toronto Press, 1962), 1. McLuhan prophetically saw deleterious effects for literature in an electronic age of illiteracy.

[2]"Champions of the King James Version feel that if God spoke English, this is how he would sound." John B. Gabel, Charles B. Wheeler, and Anthony D. York, eds., *The Bible as Literature: An Introduction,* 3d. ed. (New York, Oxford: Oxford University Press, 1996), 11.

[3]Alexander Solzhenitsyn, "Presentation Speech. Nobel Lecture, 1970" (Sect. 5 of 7). Online. *https://www.solzhenitsyncenter.org/nobel-lecture/*

[4]See Vasily Grossman, *A Writer at War: A Soviet Journalist with the Red Army, 1941-1945,* edited and translated by Antony Bievor and Luba Vinogradova, New York: Vintage Books, 2005.

[5]Gabriel García Márquez, "Introduction," in "100 Years of Pablo Neruda." April 3, 2004. Online. *https://www.democracynow.org/2004/7/16/ the_greatest_poet_of_the_20th*

[6]Pablo Neruda poem excerpt, "Let the Rail Splitter Awake," V. The Waldeen Translation, 1948. For the Spanish version of the poem, refer to Pablo Neruda, "Que despierte el leñador," VI. *Canto General, 1950. https://www. uhmc.sunysb.edu/surgery/railsplitter.html*

[7]The narrative of the funeral was taken from a tape recording of Neruda's funeral done by Carlos Ortiz Tejeda; transcribed by Ricardo Garibay; translated by Mauricio Schoijet. Reprinted by permission of University Review. Copyright 1973, Entelechy Press Corp.

[8]"A National Sonnet for Neruda, "*latimes*, 2004. *http://articles.latimes. com/2004/jun/17/world/fg-neruda17*

[9]Harold Bloom, *The Shadow of a Great Rock: A Literary Appreciation of the King James Bible* (New Haven and London: Yale University Press, 2011), 2.

[10]Samuel Beckett quoted in Denis Donoghue, *The Sovereign Ghost: Studies in Imagination* (Berkeley and Los Angeles: University of California Press), 33.

[11]Marcel Proust, I*n Search of Lost Time*, Vol. VI, *Time Regained*, translated by Andreas Mayor and Terence Kilmartin, revised by D. J. Enright (New York: Modern Library Paperback Edition, 1999), 298-99.

[12]Newton Arvin, *Herman Melville* (New York: The Viking Press, 1957), 156.

[13]Ibid., 157.

[14]Nathaniel Philbrick, *Why Read Moby-Dick?* (New York: Viking, 2011), 6.

[15]Ibid., 9.

[16]On origins of modern fiction in *Lazarillo de Tormes* see Alexander Blackburn, *The Myth of the Picaro: Continuity and Transformation of the Picaresque Novel 1554-1954*, Chapel Hill: The University of North Carolina Press, 1979.

[17]For a critical analysis of *The Woman at Otowi Crossing*, see Alexander Blackburn, *A Sunrise Brighter Still: The Visionary Novels of Frank Waters*, Athens: Swallow Press/Ohio University Press, 1991.

[18]Dylan Thomas, quoted in Andrew Sinclair, *Dylan Thomas: No Man More Magical* (New York: Holt, Rinehart & Winston, 1975), 227-29.

[19]Jackson J. Benson, *The True Adventures of John Steinbeck, Writer* (New York: The Viking Press, 1984), 121.

[20]The transcription of Faulkner's statement appears in Frederick L. Gwynn and Joseph L. Blotner, eds., *Faulkner in the University* (Charlottesville: The University of Virginia Press, 1959), 133.

[21]See John Wain, *The Living World of Shakespeare: A Playgoer's Guide*, Harmondsworth: Penguin Books, 1964, and Harold Bloom, *Shakespeare: The Invention of the Human,* New York, Riverhead Books, 1998.

[22]Joseph Conrad to William Blackwood, 31 May 1902, in *Joseph Conrad: Letters to William Blackwood and David S. Meldrum*, edited by William Blackburn (Durham: Duke University Press, 1958), 155-56.

[23]Vasily Grossman, *Life and Fate*, translated with an introduction by Robert Chandler (New York: New York Review Books, 2006), 841.

[24]Frank Waters, *People of the Valley* (Chicago: Swallow Press, 1969), 201.

[25]Percy Bysshe Shelley, "A Defense of Poetry," quoted in Julian Jaynes, *The Origin of Consciousness in The Breakdown of The Bicameral Mind* (Boston: Houghton Mifflin Company, 1976), 376.

[26]James Joyce, *A Portrait of the Artist as a Young Man* (Harmondsworth: Penguin Books, 1960), 247. The novel ends with dates: Dublin, 1904, Trieste, 1914.

[27]Ibid., 253.

[28]Leo Tolstoy, *What Is Art?* translated by Richard Pevear and Larissa Volokhonsky (Harmondsworth: Penguin Books, 1995), xviii (passage quoted in translators' Preface).

[29]Quoted from *Journal of a Novel* in Jackson J. Benson, *The True Adventures of John Steinbeck, Writer,* 672.

[30]See *Gilgamesh*, translated by John Gardner and John Maier, New York: Vintage Books, 1985. The paperback edition I read in the early 1950s, useful as a story, lacked the scholarly analysis of the poem provided by these translators.

[31]My father, William Blackburn, was a professor of English at Duke University in Durham, North Carolina, from 1926 to 1968, when he retired and went to The University of North Carolina at Chapel Hill where for two years he served as mentor to William deBuys. It was customary for Duke to sponsor concerts by famous artists. From the age of eight I accompanied my father at many of these concerts.

[32]Wikipedia is a source for "Seth Wells Cheney" references. Among his works are portraits of William Cullen Bryant and James Walker, president of Harvard. His widow, Edna Dow Cheney, became a well-known author and a prominent advocate of woman suffrage.

[33]See Louis Hyde, ed., *Rat & the Devil: Journal Letters of F.O. Matthiessen and Russell Cheney*, Hamden: Archon Books, 1978.

[34]For a full account of William Blackburn's legacy, see Alexander Blackburn, *Meeting the Professor: Growing Up in the William Blackburn Family*, Winston-Salem: John F. Blair, 2004.

[35]F.O. Matthiessen, *American Renaissance,* New York: Oxford University Press, 1941, and Leo Marx, *The Machine in the Garden*, New York: Oxford University Press, 1964.

[36]Manlio Rossi-Doria, *Centro Sociale*, nos. 57-60 (1964), 2-3.

[37]See George E. Dimock, Jr., "The Name of Odysseus," in *Homer: A Collection of Critical Essays*, edited by George Steiner and Robert Fagles (Englewood Cliffs, N.J.: Prentice-Hall, 1962), 107.

[38]The allusion is to Joanne Greenberg's *I Never Promised You a Rose Garden*, New York: Holt, Rinehart and Winston, Inc., 1964. The novel was a bestseller and made into a motion picture and song with the same title.

[39]In his notes to "Kubla Khan" Samuel Taylor Coleridge claimed that, during composition of the poem, he "was unfortunately called out by a person on business from Porlock," and was consequently unable to finish the poem, having retained but a "dim recollection of the general purport of the vision." The Person from Porlock has come to represent any interruption of a creative endeavor.

[40]John Nichols, *Dancing on the Stones: Selected Essays* (Albuquerque: University of New Mexico Press, 2000), 132.

⁴¹Marcus Aurelius, *Meditations*, translated by A.S.L. Farquhorson (New York: Alfred A. Knopf, 1992), 13.

⁴²Tony Tanner, *The Reign of Wonder: Naivety and Reality in American Literature* (Cambridge: Cambridge University Press, 1965), 7.

⁴³Ibid., 355.

⁴⁴Alexander Blackburn, *The Door of the Sad People* (Colorado Springs: Rhyolite Press, 2014), 329.

⁴⁵David Blackburn graduated from the University of Warwick, then moved to California to pursue a M.A. degree in English at UC-San Diego before devoting himself entirely to music as a songwriter, guitarist, and sound engineer. Philip Blackburn graduated from Cambridge University, then moved to Iowa to pursue a Ph.D. degree in Music at the University of Iowa. He lives in Minnesota where he is Senior Artistic Director of the American Composers Forum and Director of Innova Records. His biography, *Enclosure 3: Harry Partch (*1997) won the Deems Taylor Award presented at Lincoln Center in New York.

⁴⁶Although I have not made a thorough study of the postwar generation of English writers, John Wain was arguably the leading person of letters, given his achievements as poet, novelist, story writer, biographer and memorialist. Although honored as Oxford Professor of Poetry, following Robert Graves, Wain never won the Nobel Prize, as did William Golding, author of the best-selling *The Lord of the Flies*, but the body of Wain's work remains formidable.

⁴⁷F.L. Lucas, *Style*, 2nd ed. (London: Cassell, 1974), 112.

⁴⁸My association with Yusef Komunyakaa is described in my article, "Komunyakaa in Colorado," *Callaloo* 28:3 (2005), 491-99, Johns Hopkins University Press.

⁴⁹Iona was founded by St. Columba, who came there from Ireland in the year 543. For four centuries it was the center of Celtic Christianity. See Kenneth Clark, *Civilization: A Personal View*, New York and Evanston: Harper & Row, 1969.

⁵⁰Line 1 of "We Together" (Juntos nosotros) in Pablo Neruda, *Residence on Earth* (Residencia en la tierra), translated by Donald D. Walsh (New York: New Directions Paperback, 2004), 33.

[51]The references are to William Maxwell Blackburn, *The Architecture of Duke University*, Durham; Duke University Press, 1939, and to Henry Adams, *Mont-Saint-Michel and Chartres,* first privately printed in 1906. Adams attempts to use the century 1150-1250 as a point in history when man held the highest idea of himself as a unit in a unified universe. Since he depends upon the works of Thomas Aquinas, as he himself noted, we can assume that orthodoxy made its appeal.

[52]See George Dekker, *Sailing After Knowledge: The Cantos of Ezra Pound*, London: Routledge & Kegan Paul, 1963. Pound's "translations" from troubadour poetry and biographies form part of the poems.

[53] *The Romance of Tristan and Iseult*, as retold by Joseph Bédier, translated by Hilaire Belloc and completed by Paul Rosenfeld, New York: Vintage Books, 1945, was first produced by Bédier in 1913 in London. It is worth noting that Penguin Books brought out in 1960 Gottfried von Strassburg's *Tristan* together-er with surviving fragments of the *Tristan* of Thomas.

[54]See Denis de Rougemont, *Passion and Society*, translated by Montgomery Belgion, revised and augmented edition, London: Faber and Faber Limited, 1956, the influential American edition of which is *Love in the Western World.* Seeing in Bédier's *Tristan* of 1913 a "clue to the European mind" whereby "love is fatal, frowned upon and doomed by life itself" (p. 15), De Rougemont links the Tristan stories to "a great heresy" of "the bloody Albigensian crusade" (p. 78), thereby, in my opinion, condescending to throw love out with the holy water.

[55]Joseph Campbell, *The Masks of God: Creative Mythology* (London: Secker & Warburg, 1968), 53-59 passim.

[56]For a detailed analysis of *Lazarillo de Tormes* see Alexander Blackburn, *The Myth of the Picaro,* 26-52.

[57]Hans Meyerhoff, *Time in Literature* (Berkeley: University of California Press, 1955), 1-2.

[58]Julian Jaynes, *The Origin of Consciousness in the Breakdown of the Bicameral Mind* (Boston: Houghton Mifflin Company, 1976), 317.

[59]Wallace Stegner, *The Sound of Mountain Water: The Changing American West* (Garden City, N.Y.: Doubleday & Company, 1969), 176.

[60]From William Faulkner, *Absalom, Absalom!*, cited in this context in David Minter, *William Faulkner: His Life and Work* (Baltimore and London: The Johns Hopkins University Press, 1980), 20.

[61]Ibid., 95-97.

[62]Eudora Welty, *The Eye of the Story: Selected Essays and Reviews* (New York:Random House, 1977), 121-22.

[63]See Denis Donoghue, T*he Sovereign Ghost: Studies in Imagination* (Berkeley and Los Angeles: University of California Press, 1976), 7-10, 27-28, 68-70, 78-81.

[64]Richard Poirier, *A World Elsewhere: The Place of Style in American Literature* (New York: Oxford University Press, 1966), 6.

[65]Jay Parini, *One Matchless Time: A Life of William Faulkner* (New York: HarperCollins Publishers Inc., 2004), 5.

[66]Ibid., 1.

[67]Joseph Campbell, *The Power of Myth* (New York: Doubleday, 1988), 22.

[68]William deBuys, *A Great Aridness: Climate Change and the Future of the American Southwest* (Oxford and New York: Oxford University Press, 2011), 11. From him I have adopted the concept of "re-moralization."

[69]Ibid., 10.

[70]Ibid., 305-06.

[71]Ibid., 306.

[72]Ibid., 307.

[73]Michel de Montaigne, *The Complete Essays*, translated by M. A. Screech (New York: Penguin Books, 1991), 122.

[74]Frank Waters, "The Regional Imperative," in *Sundays in Tutt Library with Frank Waters* (Colorado Springs: The Colorado College, 1988), 50. The essay is reprinted in *Pure Waters* (Athens: Swallow Press/Ohio University Press, 2002), 121-28. Irritated by a critic's description of his work as confined by

a "regional imperative," Waters used this essay to place a prophetic emphasis upon a "planetary imperative."

[75]Pierre Teilhard de Chardin, *The Future of Man*, translated by Norman Denny (New York: Harper Torchbooks, 1969), 124.

[76]Sir Julian Huxley, Introduction to *The Phenomenon of Man* by Pierre Teilhard de Chardin (New York: Harper Torchbooks, 1961), 22.

[77]Ibid.

[78]Teilhard de Chardin, *The Future of Man*, 57.

[79]Francis Fergusson, Introduction to *Aristotle's Poetics*, translated by S. H. Butcher (New York: Hill and Wang, 1961), 4, 17.

[80]Frank Waters, *Mexico Mystique: The Coming Sixth World of Consciousness* (Athens: Swallow Press/Ohio University Press, 1989), 283.

[81]Frank Waters, *Mountain Dialogues* (Athens: Swallow Press/Ohio University Press, 1981), 7, 69.

[82]Edwin Honig, *Dark Conceit: The Making of Allegory* (New York: University Press, 1966), 53.

[83]Max Steele, Introduction to *Love, Boy: The Letters of Mac Hyman*, selected and edited by William Blackburn (Baton Rouge: Louisiana State University Press, 1969), xv-xvi.

[84]Ibid., 163. References about Andy Griffith are to be found on p. 122 and about me on pp. 130-31.

[85]Mark Anderson, *"Shakespeare" by Another Name: The Life of Edward de Vere, Earl of Oxford, The Man Who Was Shakespeare* (New York: Gotham Books, 2005), 23.

[86]Ibid., 86.

[87]"Art" in *Collected Poems of Herman Melville*, edited by Howard P. Vincent (Chicago: Packard and Company, 1947), 231.

[88]Joseph Conrad, *A Personal Record* (1912), Chap. V, in Miriam Allott,

Novelists on the Novel (London: Routledge and Kegan Paul, New York: Columbia University Press, 1959), 118-19.

[89]Harold Bloom, *The Anatomy of Influence: Literature as a Way of Life* (New Haven and London, 2011), 4.

[90]James Baldwin, quoted in Chris Hedges, review of the film "American Sniper" in *Truthdig*, 2015.

[91]See John Livingston Lowes, *The Road to Xanadu: A Study of the Ways of the Imagination*, Boston: Houghton Mifflin, 1927.

[92]See Norman Sherry, *Conrad's Western World*, Cambridge: Cambridge University Press, 1971. One reason why Nostromo is regarded as a great novel in English is that Conrad "resembled Flaubert in aiming for nothing less than an imaginative, artistic vision of life: all other views of it – political, sociological, religious – he repudiated, just as Flaubert did" (9).

[93]John Wain, *The Living World of Shakespeare,* 125.

[94]F. Scott Fitzgerald, *The Great Gatsby* (Harmondsworth: Penguin Books, 1950), 188. In any edition the words "capacity for wonder" and "green light" appear in the final four paragraphs of the novel.

[95]In the poem "Au Lecteur" in *Les Fleurs du Mal*, Charles Baudelaire identifies "Ennui"as the modern Devil. The idea remains relevant more than 150 years later.

[96]Circumnavigation of the globe and discovery of America by a Chinese fleet are well-documented in two books by Gavin Menzies, *1421* and *1434*, the latter published in New York in 2008 by William Morrow. Menzies also argues that the world maps made by the Chinese were passed on to Columbus and Magellan.

[97]Taylor Caldwell, *A Pillar of Iron* (Garden City: Doubleday & Company, Inc., 1965), 81. Beginning in 1947, Caldwell's visits to the Vatican Library in Rome provided original materials for this historical novel.

[98]Henri Troyat, *Tolstoy* (New York: Grove Press, 1967), 305.

[99]Ibid., 365-66.

[100]Ibid., 369.

[101]Ibid., 368-69.

[102]Joseph Campbell, *Myths to Live By*, New York: Viking Press, 1972, offers some examples and argumentation that I have used throughout this essay. I have supplemented his examples with some of my own, have offered a classification of the myths of war, and have added a discussion of "just" war before focusing the essay on the Atomic Age.

[103]In 1999, the NATO air war to save Kosovo was widely justified as the prevention of a humanitarian catastrophe. In the United States it was argued that "we" are debased collectively if we ignore genocidal assaults on people or refuse to make clear that the standards of human decency that we uphold aren't hollow. See especially "The Last No-Man's-Land of the Century," *The Washington Spectator* 25:10 (May 15, 1999), and "Saving People from Doom Becomes Western Policy," ibid., 25:13 (July 1, 1999).

[104]Jonathan Schell, *The Fate of the Earth* (New York: Alfred A. Knopf, 1982), 115.

[105]See Erich Fromm, *The Fear of Freedom,* London: Routledge & Kegan Paul, 1942.

[106]Joseph Campbell, *The Masks of God: Creative Mythology*, 677.

[107]For a complete discussion of these speculative matters, see Mark Anderson, *"Shakespeare" by Another Name.*

[108]G. Wilson Knight, "Time and Eternity," in *Discussions of Shakespeare's Sonnets*, edited by Barbara Herrnstein (Boston: D.C. Heath and Company, 1964), 63, 66, 70.

[109]Leslie Hotson, "Shakespeare's Sonnets Dated," in ibid., 8-21.

[110]Ralph Ellison, *Invisible Man* (New York: Second Vintage International Edition, 1995), 435-36. In any edition this passage appears in Chapter 20. Until I read this novel, I was unaware that American policemen had a history of provoking and killing young African American men.

[111]See Dean Hamer, *The God Gene: How Faith is Hardwired into Our Genes,* New York: Doubleday, 2004.

[112]Naomi Klein, *This Changes Everything: Capitalism vs. The Climate* (New York: Simon & Schuster, 2014), 314, 48, 59, 62.

[113]Chris Hedges, *Empire of Illusion: The End of Literacy and the Triumph of Spectacle* (New York: Nation Books, 2009), 38.

[114]Ibid., 44.

[115]Ibid., 52.

[116]Ibid., 103.

[117]That religions and cultures originate in myths is a theme in Yuval Noah Harari, *Sapiens: A Brief History of Humankind* (Harper, 2015), 102-03.

[118]David Ballin Klein, *The Concept of Consciousness: A Survey* (Lincoln: University of Nebraska Press, 1985), 82-83.

[119]Alberta Steinman Gilinsky, *Mind and Brain: Principles of Neuropsychology* (New York: Praeger, 1984), 84.

[120]Carl Sagan, *The Dragons of Eden: Speculations on the Evolution of Human Intelligence* (New York: Ballantine Books, 1978), 191.

[121]Alberta Steinman Gilinsky, *Mind and Brain*, 446.

[122]Ibid., 170.

[123]Ibid., 460.

[124]Ibid., 478.

ALEXANDER BLACKBURN

Alexander Blackburn was born in Durham, N. C., in 1929 and carried a passion for writing across his academic training at Yale and Cambridge and his teaching of creative writing at Pennsylvania and Colorado/Colorado Springs. For his work as educator, novelist, critic and editor he has received the prestigious Frank Waters Award for Excellence in Literature. He lives in Colorado Springs with his wife, Dr. Inés Dölz-Blackburn, Chilean-born author and Professor of Spanish and Latin American Languages and Literature.

BOOKS

The Door of the Sad People. A Novel. Rhyolite Press, 2014.

> *The Door of the Sad People* is one of the most remarkable books I have read, ever. It caught me pleasurably off guard at almost every turn. -- Fred Chappell, recipient of Yale University's Bollingen Prize for Poetry, Poet Laureate of North Carolina

---

The Voice of the Children in the Apple Tree. A Novel. Rhyolite Press, 2015.

> The atomic bomb is a turning point in world history. Both Trinc and Aeneas are closely involved in historical events, inseparable from them, and the vicissitudes they endure are terrific characterizations! *The Voice of the Children in the Apple Tree* is large, the event momentous, and the perspective always fitting. Here is another real triumph. -- Fred Chappell

---

The Cold War of Kitty Pentecost. A Novel. Swallow Press/Ohio University Press, 1979. Rhyolite Press, 2016.

> There is in it an extreme and romantic sensibility that is almost entirely missing in other contemporary writing. And *Cold War* reminds me - sadly - of how much we are missing now. There is in it discernable the influence of Faulkner and even of Wolfe, but these voices are quite amiably absolved. This is a tough, sweet, and classy book. -- Fred Chappell

Suddenly a Mortal Splendor. A Novel. Baskerville, 1995. Rhyolite Press, 2015.

Every once in a while, a good unknown writer gets anointed, the Pulitzer committee issues a prize, and sales jump. Still, for every winner there are scores of writers who are as good but are virtually unread. To that list of unknown writers, good writers toiling in obscurity, add the name of Alexander Blackburn. -- *The Dallas Morning News*

Suddenly a Mortal Splendor is elegantly built, in its leanness of thought and in the clear- lined prose that flows from a breadth of cool intelligence and warm human feeling. -- Reynolds Price, recipient of the National Book Critics Circle Award

Blackburn tears off a great hunk of late 20th century history to use as a source of inspiration and moral instruction with savage humor about man's limitless capacity for inhumanity and equally limitless capacity for survival. -- *Boston Globe*

The Myth of the Picaro. The University of North Carolina Press, 1979. UNC Enduring Editions, 2014.

Mr. Blackburn has done for the picaresque something analogous to what Empson did for the pastoral: after extracting the myth from the form, they both discover that myth is in some unlikely books. Mr. Blackburn's book bids fair to acquire something of the same enduring fame as Empson's *Varieties of Pastoral.* -- Reader's report, UNC Press

---

A Sunrise Brighter Still: The Visionary Novels of Frank Waters. Swallow Press/ Ohio University Press, 1993.

Alexander Blackburn is one of the most important writers in the American West today. -- *The Bloomsbury Review*

Waters is now on the cutting edge of just about everything we take seriously in this country: the natural environment, our socio- psychological environment, our political, ecological, and spiritual relationship to the future... Blackburn does a fine job of placing Waters within a literary context of other "visionary" writers, particularly Conrad, D. H. Lawrence, Faulkner, and Waters's beloved Melville. -- James Thomas, editor of *Best of the West*

Meeting the Professor: Growing Up in the William Blackburn Family. John F. Blair, publisher, 2004.

Meeting the Professor is one of those astounding autobiographies I've ever read. Although tender and sometimes even sweet, it also exposes the heat of the southern forge that would produce the determined westerner Blackburn became. Through that galvanizing process, Blackburn developed a national vision, worldview. His life, in short, has demonstrated the vital importance of tying regional identity with universal understanding as a method of exploring the intricacies of the human condition. -- Clay Reynolds, Director of Creative Writing, University of Texas at Dallas

Rare, indeed, is the father in American literature. Rare, too, the world of academia that escapes satire. And rarer, yet, the humble treatment of aristocrats. Here we have treatment of all three done with great tact and intelligence. -- Max Steele, recipient of the Harper Award and a founding editor of *The Paris Review*

William Blackburn possessed that subtle, ineffable, magnetically appealing quality - a kind of invisible rapture - which caused students to respond with like rapture to the fresh and wondrous new world he was trying to reveal to them. -- William Styron, recipient of the Pulitzer Prize for Fiction

---

Creative Spirit. Creative Arts Book Company, 2001.

Blackburn has collected 17 essays united by the theme of the creative spirit in literature and life. Whether discussing the picaresque novel or revolutionary discoveries in neuro- psychology, these learned but accessible essays investigate the importance of the creative writer and literature, particularly in a society in which materialism and anti- intellectualism are rampant. -- *Library Journal*

The Interior Country: Stories of the Modern West. Swallow Press/Ohio University Press, 1987. Edited with Craig Lesley.

The introduction is the best essay on the American West I've ever read. -- Frank Waters.

I like the introduction, which corroborates some notions I have held for a long time... This is a really good, various, rich collection. I'll treasure it, quote it, and plug it – Wallace Stegner, recipient of the Pulitzer Prize for Fiction.

Higher Elevations: Stories from the West: A "Writers' Forum" Anthology. Swallow Press/Ohio University Press, 1993.

Writers' Forum, 21 vols., 1974-1995, editor- in- chief.

Ranked first among non-paying, university-sponsored literary magazines by *Writer's Digest.* -- Ceil Malek

---

Gifts from the Heart: Stories, Memories & Chronicles of Lucille Gonzales Oller. University of Colorado, 2010.

Daughter of a cowboy and of a scion of one of the oldest Hispanic families in the American Southwest, "Lou," having raised a family and traveled the world, entered college at the age of 40 as a "minority re-entry woman." She was determined to realize her childhood dream of becoming a writer. And so, within a few years she found herself writing for the Colorado Springs *Gazette.* Promoted to columnist, she wrote such warmly beautiful essays – one of which was nominated for the Pulitzer Prize – that she carried a reputation as that city's voice and conscience. Upon her death in 2003 at the age of 56, she left a large legacy of stories and essays. -- Book cover

For Gifts from the Heart, a finalist for the 2010 Colorado Book Award, Blackburn gathered 60 of Gonzales's 700 columns... and several of her short stories. The result is a superb example of journalism as literature. -- *The Bloomsbury Review*

———————————————

The Fire Within: Reflections on the Literary Imagination. Irie Books, 2019.

———————————————

The Emergence of Frank Waters: A Critical Reader. Coedited with John Niza-lowski. Irie Books, Forthcoming.